CLIMATE CHANGE AND LANDSCAPE

IN THE CANADIAN ROCKY MOUNTAINS

NAT RUTTER
MURRAY COPPOLD
DEAN ROKOSH

THE BURGESS SHALE GEOSCIENCE FOUNDATION
FIELD, BRITISH COLUMBIA

SPONSORED BY THE CANADIAN SOCIETY OF PETROLEUM GEOLOGISTS

RADARSAT visualization of the Arctic Ocean

THE BURGESS SHALE GEOSCIENCE FOUNDATION

Copyright ©2006 The Burgess Shale Geoscience Foundation
P.O. Box 148, Field, British Columbia, Canada V0A 1G0
www.burgess-shale.bc.ca   info@burgess-shale.bc.ca

International Standard Book Number (ISBN) 0-9780132-1-2

Published with financial assistance from the Association of Professional Engineers,
Geologists and Geophysicists of Alberta

Contents

PREFACE

∼

News reports are full of conflicting statements about climate change. The goal of this book is to give the reader an appreciation of the major climate change in recent Earth history—from the ice age to the current interglacial conditions. To do this, we discuss the tools needed to identify climate change, how climate events are dated, examples of some of the best climate records, and the causes of climate change. We then focus on the Canadian Rocky Mountains and show how climate change has contributed to the development of the marvelous landscape that we enjoy today. We have provided ample pictures to aid the reader in identifying the features formed by glacial processes. Thus equipped to see beyond the scenery, we hope the reader will come to appreciate the temporal and spatial evolution of Earth landforms brought about by dynamic processes controlled primarily by climate change.

Witness what is happening today in the Canadian Rockies. Glaciers have been receding at historically high rates. This melting is not merely important to the scenic value; it affects the supply of fresh water to the cities, towns and farms of the prairies. Is this a result of natural climate change, or have the processes been accelerated by human activities?

We hope this book will help the reader appreciate the difficult task that scientists have in trying to decipher Earth history and predict its future. Only through an understanding of Earth history will we be able to manage intelligently our effect on the environment and predict and adjust to future climate change.

Nat Rutter
Murray Coppold
Dean Rokosh

F·

INTRODUCTION

TO QUATERNARY CLIMATE CHANGE

Climate Basics

The dynamic processes that shape and alter our world have been operating for over 4.5 billion years. One of them is climate. Climate is influenced by latitude and the circulation patterns in the oceans and atmosphere. Latitude determines the absorption of incoming solar radiation (*insolation*) that provides heat to Earth. The strongest absorption occurs in the tropics, where solar radiation strikes Earth at a near-perpendicular angle. Absorption is least at high latitudes, where the effect of insolation is tempered by its low angle of incidence. Ocean and atmospheric circulation act to redistribute heat over the surface of the globe, thus tempering the climate extremes that would exist if insolation acted alone.

Heat transport over the globe is done primarily by water, which has an immense heat capacity. Over 70 per cent of the planet is covered by ocean; only 30 per cent is land. The volume of the world's oceans is nearly 1.4 billion cubic kilometres. A seemingly small ocean warming of 0.1° C would, if that heat were transferred to the atmosphere, raise the surface temperature of Earth by 100° C. The fundamental differences between the responses of ocean and land to insolation are shown in Figure 1.

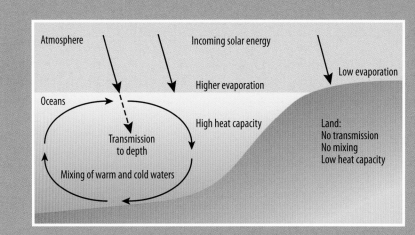

Figure 1. The different responses of land and oceans to incoming solar radiation make oceans the more effective global heat reservoir.

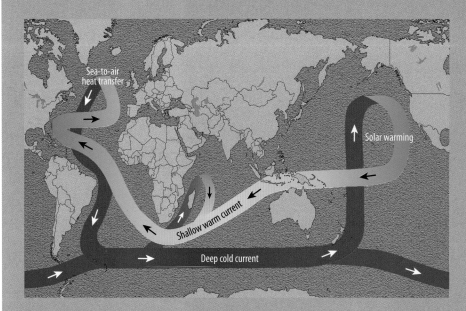

Figure 2. Shallow ocean currents (yellow and light green) transport heat from the tropics to higher latitudes. Once there, the water gives up its heat, the water cools and sinks, returning to mid-latitudes as deep ocean currents (dark green and blue).

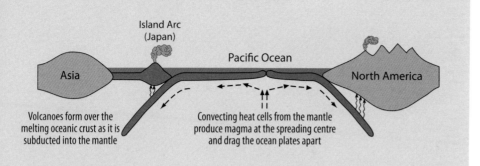

Figure 3. Schematic cross section through the Pacific Ocean illustrating the principles of plate tectonics. The light continental masses are pushed over the surface of Earth by movements of the more dense oceanic crust. Associated volcanism releases greenhouse gases to the atmosphere and affects climate.

Global ocean circulation transports heat from the tropics to high latitudes. The circulation is driven by density changes in the water mass and is called *thermohaline* circulation (Figure 2). Thermohaline refers to water density variations that arise from thermal (*thermo*) and salinity (*haline*) changes in seawater. In the Atlantic Ocean, warm and salty water from the tropics moves north toward Western Europe. Once there, it releases heat and water vapour to the atmosphere, resulting in a mild and wet winter climate in most of maritime Europe. Having given up its heat, the surface water becomes more dense and sinks to the deep ocean. It then flows south to join the Antarctic circumpolar current. The deep Antarctic circumpolar current feeds into the shallower waters of the Indian and Pacific oceans, which then flow back to the Atlantic, completing the global circuit.

PLATE TECTONICS

Both ocean and atmospheric circulation are affected by the configurations of the continents and oceans, which has not been constant through the history of the planet. With the recognition and general acceptance of the plate tectonics theory over half a century ago, has come the realization that the continents drift over the surface of the globe. These movements are driven by convective forces in Earth's interior. In brief, the convection causes new dense oceanic crust to form at spreading centres, while old seafloor is driven under the lighter, more buoyant continents and subducted back into the mantle (Figure 3). The continents are pushed about, alternately split up and amalgamated by these forces. Plate tectonics adds to the climate mix by altering greenhouse gas composition in the atmosphere (notably carbon dioxide [CO_2] released by volcanism) and weather circulation systems.

A PERSPECTIVE ON OUR WORLD

For most of the last billion years, Earth has been warmer than it is today. Some geologists recognize three climate *supercycles* in Earth history, each lasting about 400 million years and consisting of an *icehouse-greenhouse* pair (Figure 4). Icehouse conditions are favoured when the continents are massed together, as in the late Precambrian, the late Ordovician and the Carboniferous periods (Figure 5). At these times, the total length of mid-ocean spreading ridges is at a minimum, venting of CO_2 to the atmosphere is low, the greenhouse effect is reduced and cold continental weather patterns favour ice sheet formation as vast continental areas are isolated from the temperature ameliorating effect of the oceans. Greenhouse climate prevails when the supercontinents rift. The resulting long mid-ocean ridges vent much more CO_2 to the atmosphere, warming ocean waters and distributing heat to high latitudes.

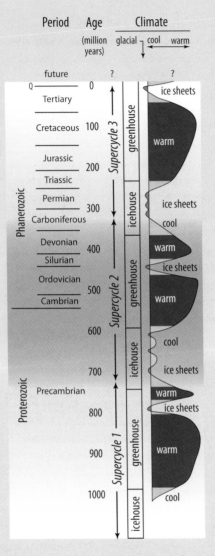

Period	Age (million years)	Climate

Climate scale: glacial — cool — warm

future — 0 — ?
Tertiary
Cretaceous — 100
Jurassic — 200
Triassic
Permian — 300
Carboniferous
Devonian — 400
Silurian
Ordovician — 500
Cambrian
— 600
Precambrian — 700
— 800
— 900
— 1000

Phanerozoic / Proterozoic

Supercycle 3 (greenhouse): ice sheets, warm
Supercycle 2 (icehouse: ice sheets, cool; greenhouse: warm, ice sheets, warm; icehouse: cool, ice sheets)
Supercycle 1 (greenhouse: warm, ice sheets; warm; icehouse: cool)

Figure 4. Climate supercycles have led to global glaciation in the past billion years. (Quaternary indicated by Q in left column.)

Quaternary ice age, 1 million years ago

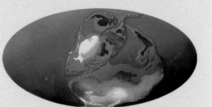

Early Carboniferous ice age, 356 million years ago

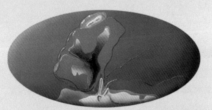

Late Precambrian ice age, 650 million years ago

Figure 5. Positions of the continents during major ice ages. Glaciation occurred on Southern Hemisphere supercontinents in the Late Precambrian (on land mass precursors to the Americas and Siberia) and Early Carboniferous (affecting southern South America and Africa). The Quaternary ice age affected the Northern Hemisphere (and Antarctica, which was already under ice due to its long residency in a polar position).

The North American continent has spent most of geologic history in tropical or sub-tropical latitudes, moving northward less than 150 million years ago. For most of its existence the average annual temperature of North America has been higher than that prevailing today.

However, global climate has been cooling for the most recent one per cent (50 million years) of geologic time (Figure 4). Antarctica has been glaciated for the last 35 million years. Canada emerged from an ice age only 10,000 years ago. Today's landscape is still adjusting to the recession of the ice. River drainage patterns and the distribution of glaciers, forest, prairie, muskeg and permafrost are all changing, and they affect the suitability of land for human habitation. Most people over 40 can attest to having experienced short term climate change in their lifetimes—be it warmer, wetter, colder, drier or other seasonal changes.

THE QUATERNARY ICE AGE

The latest glacial age, the Quaternary, is popularly known as the Great Ice Age. The Quaternary began only about 2.6 million years ago and continues today. It is characterized by alternating periods of cold climate that produce glacial advances, and warm climate that result in ice retreat. The ice age affected large parts of the high northern and southern mid-latitudes, and higher elevations even near the Equator. Presently we are witnessing an interglacial period. Continental drift has been less than 200 kilometres in 2.6 million years, too small to produce major climate shifts. So what brought on the current ice age?

A definitive answer is still uncertain. Over the last 4 million years, average global temperature has dropped 3° C. Glaciation was probably initiated by changes in the distribution of heat over Earth's surface related to the complex interplay of Earth's orbit variations, ocean and atmospheric circulation, and changes in the concentration of greenhouse gases in the atmosphere.

ORBITAL FORCING

The geometry of Earth's orbit around the Sun is not constant. There are three cyclic variations: obliquity, the tilt of Earth's axis relative to its orbital plane; eccentricity, the degree to which the orbit strays from a circle; and precession, the "wobble" of Earth's rotation axis (Figure 6). In the 1920s Milutin Milankovitch revived James Croll's 1867 idea that these orbital factors affect the seasonal and latitudinal distribution of insolation and might be enough to change Earth's climate from glacial to interglacial periods and back again. This hypothesis has come to be known as the Milankovitch theory of orbital forcing, the "pacemaker of the ice ages."

Inclination

The inclination of Earth's spin axis relative to its orbit varies between about 21.5° and 24.5° and back again about every 41,000 years. Summer occurs when the hemisphere (northern or southern) is oriented toward the Sun. The amount of tilt affects the distribution of insolation, especially at high latitudes. Higher inclination means a greater contrast in seasonal insolation; summers are warmer and winters are cooler. Less tilt means less contrast in the seasons. Warmer winters in the tropics and mid-latitudes result in an increase in the moisture supply to high latitudes and are conducive to ice and snow accumulation. Presently Earth's inclination is about 23.5° and decreasing.

Eccentricity

The eccentricity of Earth's orbit changes from near circular to slightly elliptical and back again about every 96,000 years (often referred to as the 100,000-year cycle). The point on the orbit closest to the Sun is called *perihelion* (147.5 million kilometres), while the point on the orbit farthest from the Sun is called *aphelion* (152.5 million kilometres). The change in eccentricity of the orbit is due to the gravitational influence of the Sun and the planets in the solar system, especially the massive planet Jupiter. The difference in insolation received at the outer limit of the atmosphere varies by 0.2 per cent between the circular and elliptical orbit extremes. Computer simulations of climate change, at present, suggest that this small variation in insolation is not enough, by itself, to cause Earth to change from a warmer to a colder climate.

Precession

Earth's polar axis not only varies in inclination but also wobbles like a spinning top in a movement called precession, where one complete wobble takes about 21,700 years. The result of precession is that the seasons change their position about the orbit. Presently, the northern hemisphere summer occurs at aphelion, while winter occurs at perihelion. Having the northern hemisphere winter season at perihelion, when Earth is closest to the Sun, means warmer winters and cooler summers, while the southern hemisphere experiences colder winters and warmer summers.

Result

The Milankovitch hypothesis suggests that a change in the eccentricity, tilt and precession of Earth result in a seasonal and latitudinal redistribution of the intensity of insolation on Earth. The

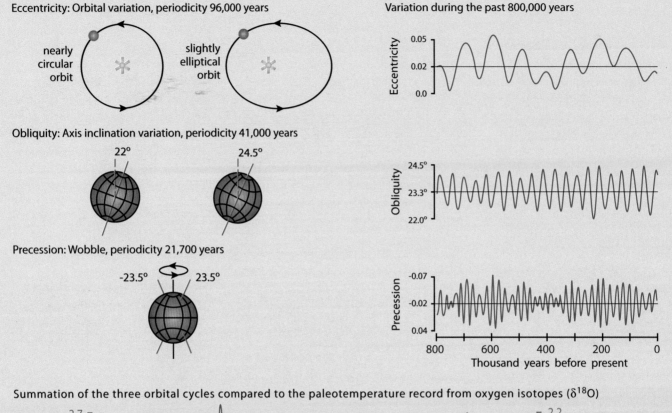

Eccentricity: Orbital variation, periodicity 96,000 years

nearly circular orbit

slightly elliptical orbit

Variation during the past 800,000 years

Obliquity: Axis inclination variation, periodicity 41,000 years

22° 24.5°

Precession: Wobble, periodicity 21,700 years

-23.5° 23.5°

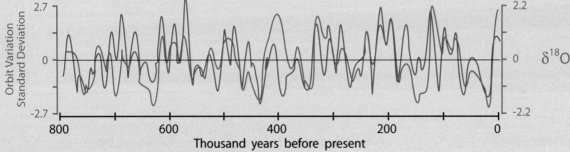

Summation of the three orbital cycles compared to the paleotemperature record from oxygen isotopes ($\delta^{18}O$)

$\delta^{18}O$

Thousand years before present

Figure 6. Earth orbit variations that influence climate. The graph at the bottom shows how the three parameters combine to affect insolation received at mid-latitudes (blue line), and the good correlation with the paleotemperature record (red line) over the past 800,000 years.

key orbital configuration to induce a glaciation is a highly elliptical orbit, with a small tilt, and winter perihelion. This results in cool northern hemisphere summers with a reduced winter/summer seasonal contrast in insolation. Since northern hemisphere winters are warmer a large amount of moisture can be supplied for glaciers to make snow and ice. Summers are cooler so that snow and ice melting will be reduced.

GRADUAL CHANGES AND THRESHOLDS

The Milankovitch variables alone are insufficient to initiate an ice age. They have been operating throughout geologic history, through warm periods and ice ages alike. Rather, orbital forcing probably interacts with other global conditions such as plate tectonics, atmospheric composition, ocean circulation, and carbon production and sequestering. Together they occasionally push climate over a threshold to produce an ice age. Over the last four million years several changes occurred to the ocean-atmosphere system. The concentration of carbon dioxide, a greenhouse gas, gradually decreased by 30 per cent. This decline promoted cooling of the air and ocean waters, especially at middle and high latitudes. As a result, the temperature of high

Figure 7. Major weather systems affecting the North American continent. The Pacific maritime polar air mass had the most effect on glaciation of the Rocky Mountains.

latitude deep water decreased and led to an increase in ocean temperature stratification.

For the western North American continent, the onset of glaciation is

probably related to temperature and circulation changes in the North Pacific Ocean (Figure 7). Water's high heat capacity means it requires more energy to heat a volume of water than a volume of air. Similarly, a water mass cools more slowly than an air mass, because there is more heat to release. Mixing of warm surface and cold deep waters within the ocean tends to reduce surface water temperature and the input of moisture to the atmosphere. However, a change occurred in North Pacific circulation beginning about 2.7 million years ago whereby mixing was inhibited and temperature stratification developed. Consequently, warm North Pacific surface waters persisted into the early winter, supplying water vapour to the weather systems moving onto the North American continent. Once over land, where the temperature-moderating effect of the warm ocean was lost, the air cooled and water dropped out as snow. This increased snowfall occurred in the midst of the general climate cooling trend that had been occurring for millions of years. Cooler summer temperatures prevented snow and ice from melting completely, leading to the onset of continental glaciation.

Once the Quaternary glaciation was initiated, it was perpetuated by long term warm-cold cycles influenced by orbital forcing. Most of Canada was glaciated several times during the last ice age. Ice periodically formed a thick, extensive ice sheet across most of northern, central and eastern Canada, whereas the mountains in the west supported their own glaciers. The effects of glaciation are strikingly evident in sculptured mountains, glacial deposits and erosional features. In areas not directly affected by overriding glaciers, signs of past severe climate are revealed by the presence of such things as fossil frost features or cold climate life forms found in temperate regions today.

ARCHIVES

OF CLIMATE CHANGE

Archives provide indirect evidence of what Earth's climate was like in the past. Archival data are compared to present-day climate data in order to estimate changes in temperature and precipitation. If numerical values cannot be estimated, relative terms like warmer, colder, wetter or drier are used. Indirect indications of climate are referred to as *climate proxy data*.

Archives of climate change can occur in almost any type of environment. This chapter presents a brief summary of some common archives of climate data and the information that can be interpreted from them.

Ocean Records

Oceans cover about 70 per cent of the planet and contain a wealth of paleoclimate (*paleo* = old) information. Long-term (a few million years) continuous records of climatic change are primarily derived from sediments that accumulate at the bottom of the ocean. Where the seafloor is a few thousand metres below the surface, erosion of bottom sediments by currents is minimized, and the archival data are most complete. These records are obtained by deep sea drilling methods that recover sediments in cores (Figure 8).

A large part of the sediment that accumulates at the bottom of the ocean comes from microscopic flora such as coccolithophores and diatoms, and fauna such as foraminifera and radiolaria. Foraminifera (Figure 9) and coccolithophores grow shells composed of calcium carbonate, while diatoms and radiolaria grow shells of silicate. These plants and animals live in the ocean under fairly selective conditions of temperature and salinity. When the plant or animal dies the shell falls to the bottom of the ocean. The remains accumulate in layers on the ocean bottom called ooze. The abundance of the different types of organisms along with their shape, size and chemical composition provides information on past ocean temperatures, ocean chemistry, ocean circulation patterns, and ocean-atmosphere interactions.

Dust particles from the atmosphere also fall into the ocean and accumulate in the ooze. Changes in the chemistry, mineralogy, grain size and abundance of the dust grains through time provide a record of changes in the intensity and direction of the winds that brought the sediment. The dust is sourced from the arid areas of the world such as the Sahara Desert of Africa and the Gobi Desert of China. Deep sea cores record changes in the aridity of the dust source areas. For example, fewer grains of desert-derived sediment in the ocean layers would suggest a reduction in the aridity of the source areas. Higher precipitation resulting in more abundant vegetation in the source will lessen erosion and reduce the amount of dust eroded by wind and transferred to the oceans. In contrast, an increase in aridity will reduce vegetation and expose desert sediment to wind erosion and transport to the ocean. (See section on Best Records.)

Figure 8. A 10-metre core of seafloor sediment, encased in a steel core barrel, being raised to the deck of the Canadian research vessel CSS Hudson.

Figure 9. Foraminifera are part of the microscopic biota recovered from deep sea cores that help scientists understand past climate.

Loess and Paleosols

Loess (pronounced *luss*) is wind blown dust composed primarily of silt-sized particles of minerals such as quartz, feldspar and mica. Loess is eroded by wind from glacial outwash, deserts, river flood plains and levees and, in modern times, from cultivated fields. When the ground is dry, large windstorms can transfer dust hundreds or even thousands of kilometres from the source areas (Figure 10). This process occurred, for example, during the dust-bowl period of the 1930s on the farmland of central North America.

Loess beds vary in thickness from a few metres to tens of metres on the plains of North America and Eurasia up to a few hundred metres in the Loess Plateau of north-central China and south-central Siberia. In each of these areas the most visible characteristic of the deposits is the alternation of grey to pinkish horizontal layers with buff to yellowish coloured horizontal layers of a few metres or a few centimetres thick (Figure 11). The grey to pinkish layers are old soils (paleosols), while the buff to yellowish coloured bands are loess beds. Each pair of alternations represents a change in climate from a relatively warm and wet period, when the soil developed, to a colder and drier climate when loess was deposited. Variation in

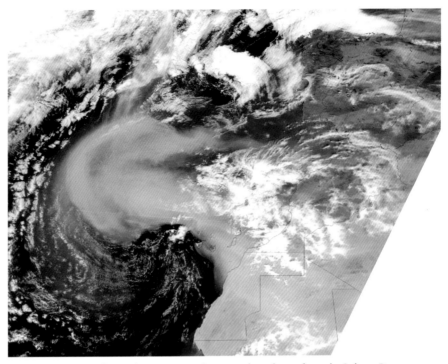

Figure 10. Intense African dust storms send massive dust plumes from the Sahara Desert out over the Atlantic Ocean (left) in this satellite view. The plume extends more than 1,600 kilometres out over the ocean. These events would create loess deposits if the sediments were deposited on land.

the size of loess grains reflects a variation in the velocity of the transporting winds. Large grains are associated with strong winds and small grains with weak winds. Thus, grain size provides information on the velocity of the prevailing winds. Likewise, changes in the type of regional soils developed in the loess may reflect variations in climate and vegetation.

Loess formation is particularly prevalent on newly deglaciated landscapes, where fine-grained material is subject to erosion before vegetation is able to spread into the area and stabilize the soil (Figure 12).

Figure 11 (below). Holocene aeolian sand and buried soils from the Lake Baikal area of eastern Russia near the border with Mongolia. The light coloured sand layers were deposited by strong winds. Darker soil horizons developed during pauses in the wind activity. The excavated section was deposited over the last 8,000 years. See Figure 47 on page 35 for an example of a modern dust storm near this area.

Figure 12 (above). The Knik River in southern Alaska forms a broad braided floodplain created by glacial meltwater that contains a high percentage of glacially-derived silt. The silt is picked up by the wind (arrow) and deposited in adjacent areas as loess.

GLACIERS

The advances and retreats of glaciers are a visible record of changes in climate from a cold to a warm period, respectively. Glaciers often leave a record of their advance in the form of moraines that consist of well to poorly sorted mixtures of boulders, cobbles, pebbles, sand, silt and clay that were eroded by the glacier. End moraines, commonly arcuate shaped, mark the furthest advance of a glacier during a certain episode. However, glaciers leave an abundance of other deposits and features that can be used to detect climate change. As we will see later, most of the climate archives in the Canadian Rockies are related to glacial features.

Glaciers are comprised of annual layers of ice and snow that record climate information back through time (Figure 13). Changes in the thickness of summer and winter layers or in the chemistry of the ice provide information on variations in the amount of precipitation in the area in the past. Additionally, the ice may contain dust or volcanic ash that has blown in from other areas, and record changes in wind direction and intensity. Probably the most important factor is that the ice contains air bubbles that capture a picture of the atmosphere at the time of ice formation. By analysing the gas within the bubbles, characteristics of the atmosphere such

as paleotemperature can be determined. More recently, human pollutants and nuclear fall-out have been detected in the ice layers.

Thus, glaciers are vast warehouses of well-dated climate change information. Ice core archives from glaciers and ice sheets from the Arctic, Antarctic and other areas have become one of the most important sources of climate information covering the last 740,000 years. (See section on Best Records.)

Figure 13. Glaciers capture annual snowfall as discrete ice layers. The chemistry of the layers provides information about paleotemperature and atmospheric composition.

Lake or Bog Sediment

Climate data in a lake or bog and the methods of its recovery are mirror images of those in the oceans (Figures 14 and 15). Sediment brought in by rivers or blown in by the wind and plant or animal remains generated within the lake drop to the bottom, forming discrete layers. The central portion of the lake (away from the effects of shoreline or river erosion) is cored to obtain a record of variations of sediments and plant and animal remains through time, which aids in the reconstruction of climate changes. If a lake dries up completely, inorganic salts will precipitate and record changes in lake level and aridity. Changes in precipitation or drainage area are recorded by variations in the shoreline level. Organic material can be radiocarbon-dated to provide the age of the sediment. More rarely, lake sediment may accumulate as annual layers, called *varves* (see section on absolute dating methods), that can be counted to provide an age for the sediment and environmental variations.

Pollen

Pollen is one of the most important archives of climate change. Anywhere there is vegetation there is the possibility of preserving pollen through time. Pollen is male genetic material from plants transferred to the female receptacle by a number of means, most notably through the air. Most plants have pollen that is unique to the genus or even species. If the pollen comes to rest in an environment where it can be preserved from oxidation, such as a lake bottom or bog, then the type and abundance of pollen provides a record of past changes in vegetation. By correlating changes in vegetation through time over a large area (e.g., North America), these changes can be correlated to changes in climate, such as those seen in ice cores. One of the most valuable uses of pollen studies (called *palynology*) is in conjunction with computer-generated climate models. The results of the climate models are compared to the past changes in vegetation in order to verify the results of the climate model. If the climate model can accurately depict past changes in climate, then we have greater confidence in its ability to predict future changes.

Figures 14 and 15. Pollen blown into small (14, above) and large (15, below) alpine lakes provides a record of vegetation and climate change.

TREE RINGS

Tree ring data are among the oldest types of paleoclimate information. Every year a tree grows a new ring around its outer perimeter, caused by seasonal differences in growth rates. In spring, growth is vigorous, producing large cells. As summer progresses into fall, growth slows and cell size decreases until it stops at the onset of winter. The result is a thicker, less dense, light-coloured summer layer (the *earlywood*) and a dense and dark winter layer (the *latewood*) (Fig 16).

When a tree is stressed due to changes in moisture or temperature, the density and thickness of the rings will vary. Tree ring width and density have been used as proxies for variations in atmospheric temperature and precipitation. However, biological processes involved in tree ring growth are extremely complex, and to determine that changes in ring width or density are due to regional climatic variation, samples must be taken over a large area.

Tree ring analysis from environments at middle latitudes like Canada is most useful because of stress placed on the plant by seasonal change in temperature and precipitation. In the tropics tree rings are less helpful because the reduced seasonal contrast results in less variation in width and chemistry.

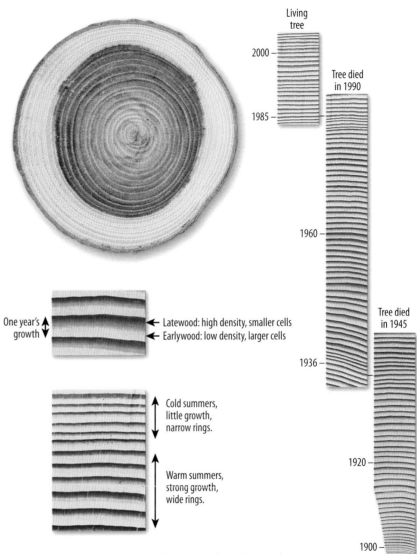

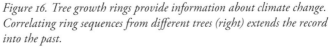

Figure 16. Tree growth rings provide information about climate change. Correlating ring sequences from different trees (right) extends the record into the past.

Trees growth rings enable dating into the past by cross-correlation, a method called dendrochronology. The sequence of growth rings can be correlated back in time from living trees to standing dead wood to buried timber by matching overlapping ring sequences found in different wood samples. In part of western North America, the record has been extended back nearly 9,000 years—almost to the end of the last ice age. Tree rings from trees growing on moraines or from stumps sheared by glaciers can be used to date glacial advances and retreats.

In addition, each ring records the prevailing level of radioactive carbon-14 in the atmosphere during that year's growth. This provides a link between dendrochronology and carbon-14 dating techniques, and has enabled scientists to calibrate the radiocarbon method so that non-wood materials can be more accurately dated (see Radiocarbon Dating). More recently, tree rings have been tested for yearly changes in geochemistry in order to derive changes in temperature and the carbon content of the atmosphere.

Speleothems

Caves can form when groundwater flows through layers of limestone (calcium carbonate) and dissolves the rock over millions of years. Later, under different chemical conditions, calcium carbonate (calcite) can be precipitated from groundwater running through the caves to form *speleothem* deposits. Speleothems occur as upward-building stalagmites, downward-building stalactites or as somewhat flat-lying flowstone (Figure 17). They capture information about changes in groundwater flow, and consequently, rainfall and atmospheric circulation.

The variation of oxygen isotopes in the calcium carbonate layers can provide information on past air temperature and therefore climate change (see section on

Figure 17. This cross-section cut through a flowstone cave deposit records changes in groundwater chemistry as successive layers were deposited. The layers can be chemically analyzed to yield proxy climate data. Millimetre scale shown at bottom of photo.

Paleotemperature, page 29.) Additional variables, including trace elements, growth rates, and organic matter content, are used to provide additional insight. The interpretation of speleothem chemistry is complicated, however, because the deposits are the result of the interplay of temperature, seasonal rainfall variation, and the nature of the rocks the water passed through on its way to forming the cave deposit. The end composition of a speleothem is not the result of a single climate variable.

The calcium carbonate may contain traces of uranium that can be used to date the speleothems. Since uranium dating techniques cover a much longer time span (400,000 years or more) than radiocarbon dating (~40,000 years), speleothems can provide well-dated climate change information for longer time periods than most other climate archives.

Coral

Corals are colonial reef-dwelling animals that build skeletons of calcium carbonate for protection (Figure 18). Coral communities grow outward and upward, precipitating layers whose thickness and density vary seasonally, controlled by changes in sea surface temperature, light intensity and the availability of nutrients.

Figure 18. Corals record climate conditions in their growth layers.

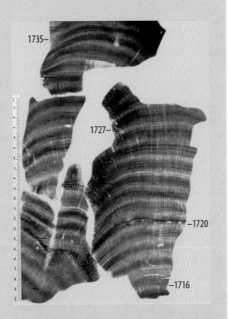

1735—

1727—

—1720

—1716

Figure 20. Fossil coral exposed in a 120,000 year old reef on Barbados.

Figure 19. Annual growth bands in a coral from the Galápagos Islands, covering the years 1716 to 1735 AD. The growth bands are more prominent in an x-ray image, seen here, than to the naked eye. Growth rate and skeleton density are sensitive to water temperature and cloud cover, and vary from winter to summer. One light-dark couplet represents one year's growth. Rapid coral growth in the fall and winter deposits low density skeletal material (light bands), whereas slower summer growth results in higher density calcite (darker bands). Investigator's correlation marks are noted on photo. Millimetre scale on left edge.

The thickness variations of layers in coral skeletons, and the oxygen isotopes and trace element ratios they contain, are indicators of paleotemperature, paleoclimate and salinity. Calibration is obtained by correlating modern coral growth bands to records of temperature and precipitation from the same general area. Modern growth rates can be compared to banding in fossil corals to extract paleoclimate information.

Most shallow water corals grow in the tropical oceans. They provide climate information that is complimentary to that from terrestrial mid-latitude tree rings, and help link global climate changes.

Coral skeletons, similar to speleothems, may contain traces of uranium that can be used to date the coral. Modern corals provide continuous records up to about 400 years (Figure 19). Fossil corals provide similar short time interval windows going back to about 130,000 years (Figure 20).

INSECTS

Insects, the dominant class of animal on Earth, are found in a variety of environments. When the insects die, their exoskeletons are used to identify the species. Coleoptera (beetles) and some flies are particularly sensitive to climate changes (Fig 21). Climate

Figure 21. Beetles are sensitive to climate change. Carabus vietinghoffi *(shown here) occurs in northern latitudes including Alaska and the Northwest Territories of Canada.*

information is obtained by comparing the modern distribution of insects to paleo-distributions of the same species. If the insect distribution has changed, then perhaps the environment that preserves the insect also changed. Similar to pollen studies, a critical aspect of this archive is to preserve the remains. The most common environments that preserve exoskeletons are oxygen-depleted environments such as lakes and peat bogs.

Two key assumptions, however, are that the modern assemblage of insects tolerates climatic change in the same manner as the paleo-assemblage and that there are no other influences that can cause the change in distribution. This is not always the case, however, since human disturbance or a change in the genetic make up of the insect could cause a population of insects to migrate, irrespective of the climate. In all case studies, extreme care is taken to isolate climate as the main factor in change.

MIDDENS

Fossil middens are nests built by packrats (Figure 22). The nests are composed of flora from the local area encased in crystallized packrat urine. Examining a number of old nests over an area provides a record of changes in vegetation, and radiocarbon dating gives the timing of change. Packrat nests are commonly well preserved in caves and rock shelters in the southwest U.S. and in other dry areas.

HISTORICAL RECORDS

Historical records provide evidence of climate change based on weather observations going back through recent centuries. Observers have recorded phenomena such as spring and fall frost dates, the appearance and duration of snow, spring flowering dates of common plants, and periods of heavy rainfall or drought. Historical records go back

Figure 22. A 12,000 year old packrat midden from the Sonoran Desert in Arizona. Needles of a singleleaf piñon (Pinus monophylla) *are well preserved and clearly visible. Coin provides scale.*

several hundred years in Europe and several thousand in China. In Canada, there are few records of climate before the 1800s.

Historical records are usually contained in diaries or in the journals of scientists, but they are also recorded in paintings or drawings (Figure 23). Accurate temperature measurements, based on the mercury thermometer, became available only about 300 years ago. Widespread temperature recordings go back less than 200 years, and coverage is sparse over most of the globe. Interpretation of non-rigorous observations is complicated by the human tendency to record unusual conditions and to ignore the normal.

One particularly rich data source resides in the log books of 18th and 19th century sailing ships of the European maritime nations. The logbooks provide enough data to give a daily picture of conditions in the Atlantic and Indian oceans. They cover the immediate pre-instrumental period between 1750 and 1854, and are the only source of widespread systematic data for the oceans in that period. Using the routes, travel times, and observations of wind speed, direction, precipitation and ice cover which were made at least thrice daily (Figure 24), investigators can map past changes in ocean currents and winds. These data can be compared with modern records to look for short-term changes in ocean circulation that affect climate.

Figure 23. A painting by the Flemish master Pieter Bruegel the Elder, depicting activities on a frozen pond in Holland in 1565, a European winter experience rarely seen today.

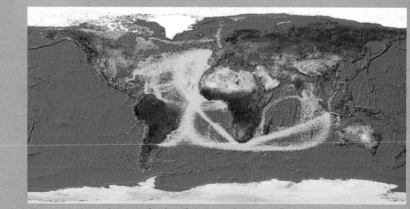

Figure 24. Map showing the distribution and density of meteorological observations from ships' log books between 1750 and 1854.

Time Period (years)

Climatic or Environmental Interpretation

Climate Archive Repository	1	10	100	1,000	10,000	100,000	1,000,000	10,000,000	Measurements taken	Temperature	Precipitation	Air chemistry	Water chemistry	Vegetation	Ice extent	Volcanism	Magnetic field	Sea/Lake level	Solar activity	Treeline
Ocean Sediment									Biota type and abundance. Mineralogy and chemistry of fossils and sediment. Grain size.											
Paleosols									Soil type and chemical composition. Pollen type and abundance.											
Loess									Sediment mineralogy and grain size. Chemical and magnetic properties.											
Glaciers (Ice Cores)									Physical properties of ice. Atmospheric chemistry from trapped air. Chemistry of included particles.											
Glacial Deposits									Moraine size, composition.											
Tree Rings									Ring width, density and isotopic composition.											
Lake and Bog Sediments									Grain size, chemical and magnetic properties of sediment. Type and abundance of biota.											
Pollen									Pollen type and abundance.											
Speleothems									Cave deposits. Air temperature, chemistry and age.											
Coral									Reef coral growth patterns. Species distribution and abundance.											
Insects									Species distribution and abundance.											
Middens									Fossil flora.											
Historical									Written records.											

Figure 25. Summary of climate archives and their use in paleoenvironment interpretation.

DATING

THE ARCHIVES

Only through well-dated sequences of climatic events will we understand the distribution, duration, mechanisms and frequencies involved in climate change. There are several dating methods that can be employed, but unfortunately there are inherent limiting factors in all of them, as well as a scarcity of suitable dating material found in nature. Some of the more important methods are discussed in this chapter.

RADIOACTIVITY

All matter is composed of atoms. Atoms consist of a nucleus containing positively-charged protons and electrically neutral neutrons, surrounded by an orbiting cloud of negatively-charged electrons (Figure 26). The number of protons gives the atom its chemical identity as an element. For example, the carbon nucleus contains six protons, nitrogen contains seven and oxygen eight. A change in the number of protons changes the chemical identity of the element.

The total number of protons and neutrons in an element is called the *atomic mass*. Thus oxygen, with eight protons and eight neutrons has a mass of 16. The number of neutrons in an element can vary slightly to create varieties of the element, called isotopes. Thus, oxygen can exist with a nucleus comprised of eight protons and eight neutrons, or eight protons and ten neutrons. These isotopes are indicated by the notation ^{16}O and ^{18}O to indicate the different masses.

Like charges repel. The repelling effect between protons in the nucleus is counteracted in two ways—by the presence of neutrons and by an overall cohesive energy. Neutrons contribute to stability by diluting the repulsive forces between protons. The actual mass of a nucleus is always slightly less than the sum of the individual protons and neutrons. The mass of ^{16}O is 15.9994 rather than 16. The reason is that some of the mass has been changed into energy—the energy needed to form the nucleus and keep its particles together. This energy is called *binding energy*, and the higher the binding energy the more stable the nucleus.

Binding energy increases as the atomic mass increases, up to atomic masses of about 60. It slowly decreases thereafter for higher masses. Elements with large masses and lower binding energy are unstable, and to reach a more stable state they undergo spontaneous decay, emitting nuclear particles and high energy radiation. These elements are said to be *radioactive*. For example, uranium 238 has 92 protons and 146 neutrons for a total mass of 238. ^{238}U decays to ^{234}Th (thorium) by emitting two protons and two neutrons.

How fast do radioactive atoms decay? There is no way of predicting when an individual atom will decay. Therefore, scientists use a bulk measure called half life. Half life is the time it takes for half the atoms of a radioactive element to decay (Figure 27). This measure is unique to each element. For example, ^{238}U has a half life of 4.5 billion years, ^{14}C (a radioactive isotope of carbon) 5,730 years, and ^{131}I (iodine) 8 days. This means that half the uranium present at the formation of the Earth 4.5 billion years ago has disappeared and, of course, there is no original iodine-131 or carbon-14.

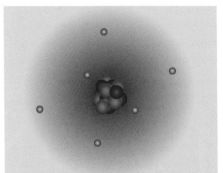

Figure 26. Composition of an atom—carbon has six protons (red) and six neutrons (green) in the nucleus and an orbiting cloud of six electrons (blue).

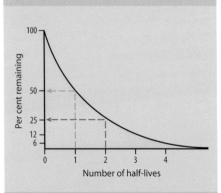

Figure 27. Radioactive decay and the concept of half life.

RADIOCARBON DATING

By far the most important dating method for the last ice age is radiocarbon or carbon-14 dating. It is based upon the known rate of decay of ^{14}C, a radioactive isotope of carbon that is produced in the Earth's atmosphere. Cosmic rays, originating from outer space, bombard nitrogen atoms (^{14}N) in the air and knock a proton out of the nucleus, changing the element to carbon-14 (Figure 28). The newly made ^{14}C atoms react quickly with oxygen to form carbon dioxide (CO_2) while still in the atmosphere, and are then taken up by plants through photosynthesis. Animals subsequently acquire ^{14}C by eating plants. Upon death, no new radiocarbon is incorporated in plant tissues or animal skeletons. The radiocarbon decays back to stable ^{14}N at a known rate, the half-life, which is 5,730 years. As the ^{14}C decays, the total amount of radioactivity in the sample decreases. By comparing the radioactivity of the sample with that of the atmosphere, it is possible to compute how many half-lives have passed, and therefore the age of the sample.

There are two main methods for determining the number of ^{14}C atoms in a sample, one indirect and the other direct. The indirect method (the conventional method) is to calculate the amount of ^{14}C atoms present in a sample by measuring

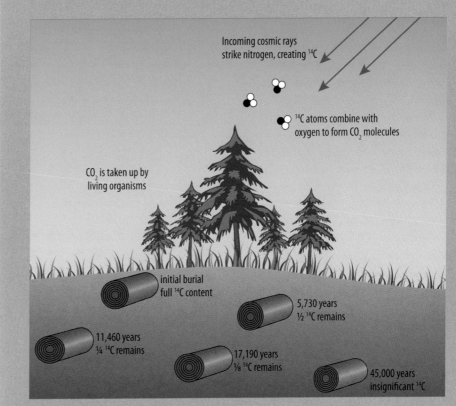

Figure 28. Production of radiocarbon and its decay in organic material.

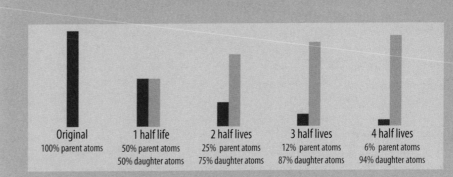

Figure 29. Parent-daughter ratios change with successive half-lives.

the amount of ^{14}C radioactivity (that is, the amount of beta decay). The more direct method is accomplished by counting the number of ^{14}C atoms present in a sample, relative to ^{12}C, using a mass spectrometer instrument. This technique, called accelerator mass spectrometry (AMS), can use a smaller amount of sample to count the number of ^{14}C atoms present with accuracy equal to the conventional method.

After about ten half-lives, the amount of radioactivity remaining in a sample is very small (Figure 29). Therefore, the maximum age of a sample that can be dated by the radiocarbon method is about 40,000 years.

Caution must be taken to ensure the sample dated has not been contaminated by older material (depleted in ^{14}C) or younger material (enriched in ^{14}C). Also, the production of ^{14}C in the atmosphere has not been constant and this variation has to be accounted for through calibration with other dating methods, notably tree rings. Raw radiocarbon dating of samples older than about 2,500 years gives ages that are too young due to atmospheric ^{14}C variation. Researchers use corrections that convert "radiocarbon years" into calendar years (Figure 30). All carbon dates mentioned in this book are adjusted to represent approximate calendar years.

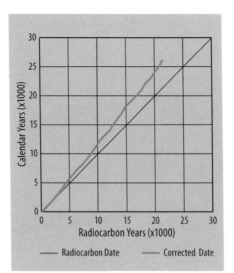

Figure 30. Generalized correction chart for radiocarbon dates. Corrections for marine and terrestrial samples differ from each other.

URANIUM-SERIES DATING

Naturally occurring radioactive elements such as uranium have isotopes that decay at known rates into other elements (called daughter elements). The proportion of parent to daughter elements in a sample tells us the number of half-lives that have occurred, which is used to find the age of the sample. Equal amounts of parent and daughter elements mean one half-life has passed. If there are three times as many daughter atoms as parent atoms, then two half-lives have passed (Figure 29). The age of the sample is calculated by assuming that the sample initially contained only parent atoms, and that there was no

loss or gain of daughter atoms since the rock or mineral was formed. However, if daughter atoms were initially present in the rock, a correction can be made.

Uranium-series dating is based upon decay products of uranium-238 and uranium-235. The number of parent and daughter atoms presently in a sample can be measured using a mass spectrometer, as in carbon dating. Uranium series dating is particularly useful for dating cave deposits as far back as 400,000 years.

FISSION TRACK DATING

Minerals such as apatite and zircon contain small amounts of uranium, present as the isotopes ^{235}U and ^{238}U. Uranium-238 atoms trapped in minerals undergo spontaneous fission, in which the nucleus splits into two fragments. The fragments are ejected into the surrounding mineral crystal lattice, creating damage tracks called fission tracks (Figure 31). The tracks accumulate at a constant rate called the decay rate. The number of tracks on a polished mineral surface is counted, using a high power optical microscope, and the density of tracks in a volume of sample can be computed.

The number of tracks in a sample is a function of the initial concentration of U-238 and increases with age. Since

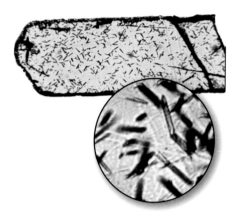

Figure 31. Fission tracks in an apatite crystal about 2 mm long. Inset shows detail of etched tracks. Each track is about 15 microns (0.015 mm) in length.

heat promotes the healing of fission damage, the tracks represent the time since the mineral cooled below its healing temperature, approximately 120° C for apatite and 200° C for zircon. The tracks are subtle, but etching in dilute nitric acid enhances their visibility.

Dating by this method covers a wide range of materials, from archaeological objects to minerals up to two billion years in age, as long as the mineral has remained below the track healing temperature. This method is commonly used to date volcanic ash layers, some of which are found in western Canada.

Thermoluminescence (TL) and Optical Stimulated Luminescence (OSL) Dating

Radiation given off by radioactive minerals (e.g., uranium) in the rock frees electrons to move through the crystal lattice or structure of the luminescent material, and some are trapped in imperfections in the crystal structure. These electrons are locked in the trap under normal temperatures. Subsequent heating of the crystal, up to about 500° C, releases the trapped electrons, resulting in an emission of light. This process is known as *thermoluminescence* (*thermo* = heat; *luminescence* = light). Suitable materials are clay pottery, calcite, diamonds, quartz or feldspar minerals.

The amount of thermoluminescence is proportional to the total accumulated dose of radiation after burial. It is a function of the natural rate of radiation from radioactive minerals (the dose rate) and the length of time that the sample has been radiated (the absolute age). The age of a sample is determined by measuring the total accumulated dose and dividing by the dose rate (per year) determined from the sample or at the sample site. OSL dating is similar to TL dating except that a light source is used to excite the sample, resulting in luminescence.

For TL or OSL dating to be possible the sample must be *zeroed*. That is, the sample must first have undergone some kind of event such as heating or exposure to sunlight which erased any previous exposure to radiation prior to burial. Wind blown material such as loess is ideal for TL and OSL dating because exposure to sunlight as the particles are transported in the atmosphere resets the clock by removing previously trapped electrons from the crystals. Upon deposition and exclusion from sunlight, loess begins again to accumulate a natural dose of radiation. The age range of this method is from about 2,000 to about 200,000 years.

Surface Exposure Dating

Cosmogenic radiation emanating from outer space impacts the surface of the Earth and can produce isotopes such as chlorine-36, helium-3 and beryllium-10 in exposed rocks. Quartzites (sandstones consisting almost entirely of quartz grains) are particularly well suited to surface exposure dating because their simple chemistry allows the isotopes to be recorded more easily. The amount of isotope present is proportional to the rate of cosmogenic radiation. Similar to TL and OSL dating, the age is derived in the time since the material was first exposed. The upper age limit for these techniques is approximately 700,000 years for ^{36}Cl, 1 million years for ^3He and 3 million years for ^{10}Be. Although there are problems with this method, it is being used more and more to date the ages of surfaces newly exposed by deglaciation, such as bedrock and large glacial erratics. Fortunately, quartzite is an abundant rock type in the main ranges of the Canadian Rocky Mountains. This method has been successful in determining when large quartzite boulders were deposited on the surface of glacial deposits in the plains east of Calgary, 15,000 to 20,000 years ago.

LICHENOMETRY

Lichens are composed of algal and fungal communities that live together symbiotically. Lichens require sunlight, and many obtain their nutrients from minerals on stable rock surfaces. Following a glaciation, rocks that were underneath the ice become exposed and are colonized by lichens. Lichen growth rates are species dependent, and are affected by changes in climate and by different types of substrate on which the lichens live. Growth rates are obtained by measuring a large number of maximum lichen sizes on material of known age such as gravestones and historic or prehistoric buildings, or on natural surfaces whose exposure time is known. Lichenometry is based on the assumption that the largest lichen growing on a

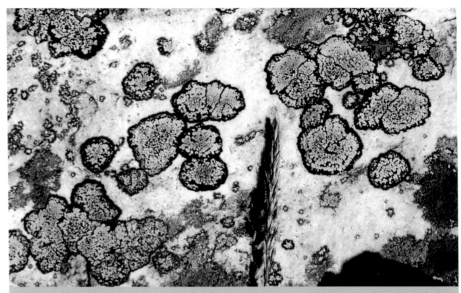

Figure 32. Rhizocarpon geographicum *colonies growing on a Cambrian quartzite boulder in Banff National Park. The central portion of the lichen is a mix of fungus and the alga* Trebouxia. *The lichen grows by extending a black fungus perimeter which is then colonized by the alga.*

rock is the oldest individual. However, lichenometry provides a minimum age only, since there is a delay between the time a rock is exposed and the time that it is colonized by lichens, and large colonies may interfere with each other, slowing their growth rate.

Rhizocarpon geographicum is the familiar crustose, yellow-green lichen that grows on quartzite (sandstone) boulders in the Rockies (Figure 32). *R. geographicum* patches grow at between 0.02 and 2 millimetres per year, with the higher rates occurring in the early growth phase. It is the lichen commonly used for dating in western Canada. Lichens can provide absolute dating of surfaces 500 years old or less, such as more recent glacial moraines. Beyond that, the slowing growth rate and interference between colonies restrict lichen use to relative dating.

VARVES

A *varve* is a couplet of relatively coarse material, usually silt, and clay deposited annually in a lake or other body of standing water. During the summer, when the lake is ice-free and material from streams (usually glacial streams) and other sources is brought in, wind, currents and water density variation in the lake keep the clay in suspension, whereas the coarser material is deposited. During the winter when the lake surface is frozen, isolating the water column from wind and currents, the clay slowly settles out. Thus a couplet of coarse material and clay represents one year of deposition. If a reference age can be established by absolute or relative dating, then counting the varves above and below the reference point can give a continuous record of changes in sedimentation through time. Varve records extending as far back as 10,000 to 11,000 years have been identified in Scandinavia, northern Canada and parts of the northern United States.

OTHER METHODS OF ABSOLUTE DATING

Other specialized dating methods, such as electron spin resonance and amino acid racemization, are not commonly utilized in western Canada.

EXTRACTING

CLIMATE INFORMATION

This chapter explains the use of oxygen isotope data, arguably the most important tool in determining paleotemperature, and reviews some of the longest and best-dated climate change records from around the world.

PALEOTEMPERATURE

There are two isotopes of oxygen. ^{16}O, with eight protons and eight neutrons is the most common form; ^{18}O is an isotope containing two extra neutrons. Overall, ^{16}O is 500 times as abundant as ^{18}O, but the ratio can vary in different environments. In order to quantify this variation, a reference standard has been defined, and a particular oxygen isotope ratio is expressed as the excess of ^{18}O over that in the reference. This difference or "delta" is noted as $\delta^{18}O$.

Seawater contains both isotopes in its water molecules. Over the open ocean ^{16}O evaporates preferentially because it is lighter, and some of the heavier ^{18}O that does evaporate rains out quickly. The change is small but measurable. On average, for every 10 metres of seawater evaporated, the ocean $\delta^{18}O$ rises by 1/10,000. The evaporation rate depends on temperature. The colder the air, the lower the amount of ^{18}O entering the atmosphere. Marine organisms build their skeletons from seawater, and fossils retain the prevailing oxygen isotope ratio, which can be analyzed to determine paleotemperature.

When the water vapour moves over land and precipitates as rain or snow, it is enriched in ^{16}O. In glacial ice, $\delta^{18}O$ reflects the surface temperature at the site of deposition. In a glacial period, the ocean has a low $\delta^{18}O$ and land ice has a more negative $\delta^{18}O$ (Figure 33). The alternations of $\delta^{18}O$ in ocean and ice cores provide records of glacial and interglacial periods.

The most direct indication of climate change in ice cores comes from the study of the chemical composition, including oxygen isotopes, of minute air bubbles trapped in the ice. Snow crystals can contain air bubbles as inclusions (Figure 34). When snow falls on the glacier and becomes compressed to form ice, air bubbles between snow crystals become trapped in the layers. The chemical composition of the air bubbles is a record of the composition of the Earth's atmosphere at the time of deposition.

BEST RECORDS

Now that we have examined some of the archives, or proxy records, of climate change let's look at some of the best records. We have chosen three records that are from rather diverse environments. The first record is comprised of ice cores from Greenland and Antarctica that span the last 740,000 years. The second

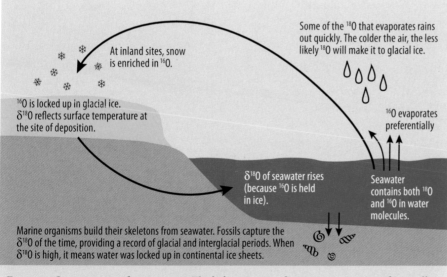

Some of the ^{18}O that evaporates rains out quickly. The colder the air, the less likely ^{18}O will make it to glacial ice.

At inland sites, snow is enriched in ^{16}O.

^{16}O is locked up in glacial ice. $\delta^{18}O$ reflects surface temperature at the site of deposition.

^{16}O evaporates preferentially

$\delta^{18}O$ of seawater rises (because ^{16}O is held in ice).

Seawater contains both ^{18}O and ^{16}O in water molecules.

Marine organisms build their skeletons from seawater. Fossils capture the $\delta^{18}O$ of the time, providing a record of glacial and interglacial periods. When $\delta^{18}O$ is high, it means water was locked up in continental ice sheets.

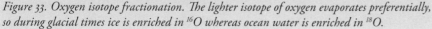

Figure 33. Oxygen isotope fractionation. The lighter isotope of oxygen evaporates preferentially, so during glacial times ice is enriched in ^{16}O whereas ocean water is enriched in ^{18}O.

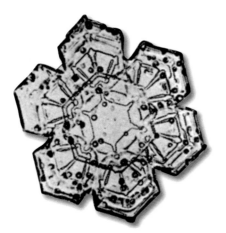

Figure 34. *Air bubbles contained in snowflakes capture the atmospheric composition.*

record comes from sediment deposited in the Atlantic Ocean, and the third record consists of alternating loess and paleosols from the Loess Plateau of north-central China. Both the Atlantic Ocean and Chinese records span approximately the last 2.6 million years. Neither of these records gives as much detail on climate change as the ice core records, but they are valuable for studying the trends in climate over a much longer period of time.

MODERN ICE SHEET CORES

Since the mid-1990s ice cores from Greenland and Antarctica have provided the most valuable records of climate change. Ice sheet coring is a technological

feat. The cores are over 3,000 metres in length and took years to drill, as they were recovered in short lengths of a few metres at a time (Figure 35). The data are very useful because the ice cores have a built-in dating method in the form of annual ice layers. Thus, climate changes recorded in the ice core data can be examined with a high degree of temporal precision (Figure 36).

The first Greenland cores extended back 105,000 years, but did not reach the record of the last interglacial at 120,000 years since the bottom layers of the core were structurally disturbed by glacial flow. Coring in North Greenland from 1996 to 2003 finally obtained a core in which individual years are distinguishable (Figure 37) extending back 123,000 years.

In Antarctica the precipitation is lower and the ice layers are condensed, so single years cannot be seen. The 3,623-metres Vostok ice core recovered in 1998 extended the record back 420,000 years through four glacial cycles. In 2004, the Dome C core drilled in East Antarctica obtained a 3,139-metres core reaching back 740,000 years and recording eight glacial cycles. It has the potential to reach 800,000 to 900,000 years if drilling can be conducted to bedrock and the basal layers are intact.

Figure 35. *Studying an ice core is cold work. A scientist extrudes an ice core from the coring equipment.*

Figure 36. *Researchers study a slabbed ice core from Greenland. This core is rich in annual dust bands and air bubbles that create cloudiness in the ice.*

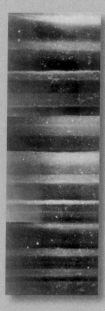

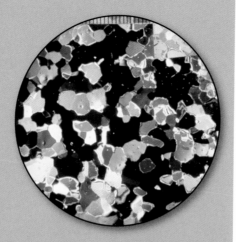

Figure 37 (left). A 19 cm long ice core from 1,855 metres depth in the Greenland GISP-2 borehole, illuminated from behind. Eleven years are represented by light summer and dark winter ice couplets.

Figure 38 (above). When a thin wafer of ice is viewed through a microscope using cross polarized light, the crystal structure becomes evident. This sample, from 333 metres depth in the GISP-2 borehole, shows ice crystals trapping air bubbles as small round inclusions. Scale in millimetres.

natural temperature changes. A series of relatively short-lived cold and warm periods are present, each lasting roughly 1,000 years. One of the most studied intervals in this core and in other climate records around the world is a cold period called the Younger Dryas. (See section on Short Term Climate Change). In the ice core, the Younger Dryas interval occurred from about 13,000 to 11,600 years ago. The data indicate a return to near full-glacial climate. One of the most striking pieces of information regarding the Younger Dryas is the rapidity of the natural change. The ice core data indicate that the onset and termination of the Younger Dryas cold period may have occurred in as little as 5 to 20 years, with a temperature change as much as 10° C.

Ice cores include a chronicle of past changes in temperature, precipitation, composition of the lower atmosphere, volcanic eruptions, pollution and a variety of other climate indicators. All of these can be studied in detail because of the annual ice layers. We'll briefly look at three climate archives from the ice core: the oxygen isotope content of the ice, the chemical composition of bubbles trapped in the ice (Figure 38) and variations in the dust content of the ice.

The oxygen isotope content of ice layers indicates that a cold period (the last glaciation) occurred from about 75,000 to about 11,000 years ago (marine isotope stages 4 through 2, Figure 39). This is the last glacial period, called the Wisconsinan. Within it there were several sub-cycles of warmth and cold. The maximum cold temperatures occurred at about 20,000 and 68,000 years ago when the climate was 10-15° C colder than at present. At the end of the cold period, the temperature warmed and the variability in temperature was small relative to that of the glacial period. The oxygen isotope record during the last glaciation, however, shows marked variability in

Air bubbles can be sampled for the concentration of carbon dioxide (CO_2) and methane (CH_4), both greenhouse gases (Figure 40). There is a good correlation between an increase in these gases and a warming of the atmospheric temperature, and conversely during cold periods the content of these gases in the air bubbles is much lower. From about 20,000 years ago to the present the atmospheric content of CO_2 changed from about 180 parts per million by volume (ppmv) to 280 ppmv by 1800, and to about 380 ppmv at present.

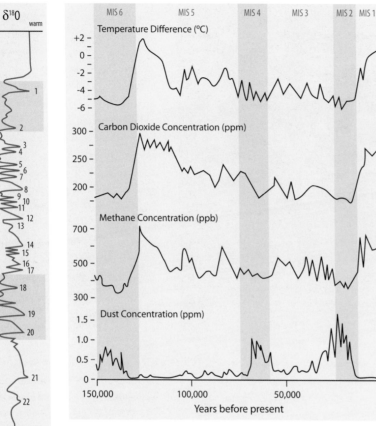

Figure 40 (above). Paleoclimate information for the past 150,000 years extracted from ice layers and air bubbles in the Antarctic Vostok core. The temperature curve for the last glacial-interglacial period (marine oxygen isotope stages 1 to 5, denoted MIS) is derived from the concentrations of carbon dioxide and methane. The dust measurement is highest in cold periods when more land is exposed due to lowered sea level and vegetation is reduced, allowing winds to transport fine particles onto the ice.

Figure 39 (left). Variation in oxygen isotopes in a Greenland ice core (GISP2) records temperature variations over the last 110,000 years. Marine isotope stages noted in red. Brief periods of relative warmth occurring within major cycles are indicated by small figures on curve.

Dust is also found in the ice layers deposited along with snow. Dust forms the nuclei around which water vapour condenses. An increase in dust in the atmosphere is generally considered to have a cooling effect on the planet by blocking the penetration of incoming sunlight (insolation). Variations in the amount of dust in the ice core reflect the concentration of dust in the atmosphere. The ice core layers clearly show an increase in the concentration of dust during cold periods. The dust that fell on the Greenland ice sheet was brought from arid areas in other parts of the world, such as the deserts of China.

OCEAN SEDIMENT RECORDS

Grain Size

Deep sea cores can be analyzed for a variety of climate information (Figure 41). Billions of tons of sediment accumulate in the ocean basins each year, and its nature and abundance provides information on climatic conditions. Horizons of coarse material (gravels) in fine-grained deep sea sediments indicate sediment transport by icebergs, corresponding to times of increased glacial activity (Figure 42). Volcanic ash layers provide information about the intensity and direction of wind blowing from the land areas to the oceans. However, the most important proxy is the occurrence of foraminifera.

Figure 41. A scientist examines a deep sea core that has been sliced in two to reveal fresh material undamaged by drilling.

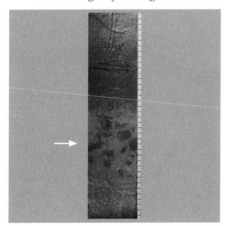

Figure 42. A deep sea core containing ice-rafted gravels (arrow) dropped into fine-grained sediment. Centimetre scale.

Figure 43. A sample of Holocene deepwater ooze from a North Atlantic core. The fine mud has been washed away, leaving a residue comprised mostly of foraminifera.

Foraminifera as Temperature Indicators

Foraminifera are tiny single-celled animals that live in the oceans, either suspended in the upper 200 metres of the water column (planktonic) or on the sea floor (benthonic). The soft tissue of the foraminfer is enclosed in a protective shell made of secreted calcite or of inorganic particles stuck together (agglutinated) by the animal. As the animal grows it forms successively larger chambers in which

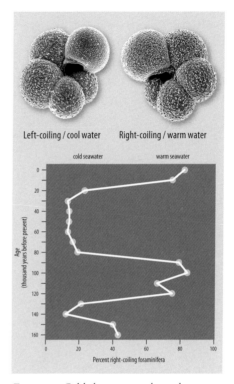

Figure 44. Cold climate periods can be distinguished from warm by counting the populations of right- and left-coiling Neogloboquadrina pachyderma in samples of sediment recovered from deep sea cores.

to live. These are often added in a spiral fashion. Many foraminifera species are environmentally sensitive, preferring particular water temperatures or salinities. Upon death of the organisms, the shells sink to the sea floor and form part of the sediment (Figure 43).

Planktonic Foraminifera

Water temperature affects planktonic foraminifera as they adopt shell features that reflect buoyancy requirements and the need to protect their shells from dissolution. Some foraminifer species respond to temperature by coiling their shells in different directions.

Neogloboquadrina pachyderma is one such foraminifer. When the Earth experiences periods of relatively cold temperatures (a glacial period), shallow ocean waters are cooler and *N. pachyderma* builds a shell that coils to the left. Alternatively, during periods of relatively warm ocean temperatures (an interglacial) *N. pachyderma* builds a shell that coils to the right. The appearance or disappearance of these right or left coiling animals marks the change in water temperature (Figure 44). Thus, by counting the number of right coiling and left coiling animals in a sample, we get an indication of the general temperature of the shallow ocean water. In a given area, if right-coiling species dominate, then the surface water was warmer; more left coiling species and the surface water of the ocean was cooler.

Benthonic Foraminifera

Deep ocean water is insulated from surface temperature fluctuations, and maintains a temperature close to 0° C.

Figure 45. The loess plateau of north-central China contains deposits over 300 metres thick.

Nevertheless, slow oceanic circulation ensures water molecules are exchanged between the surface and deep ocean.

Benthonic foraminifera withdraw oxygen from the surrounding water to secrete their shells. Water from a glacial period is enriched in ^{18}O (see discussion of the oxygen cycle, page 29) and as a result so are benthonic foraminifer shells. Figure 48A (page 38) shows the warm and cold periods for the last 2.6 million years, based on variations of $\delta^{18}O$ in a North Atlantic Ocean core. This is just one record out of hundreds of deep sea cores recovered from the world's oceans.

CHINESE LOESS/PALEOSOL RECORDS

China is the most populous country in the world and is well known for the longevity of its civilization. What is less well known is its outstanding record of climate change that reaches back at least 2.6 million years.

The climate record is hidden in massive blankets of wind blown loess, covering

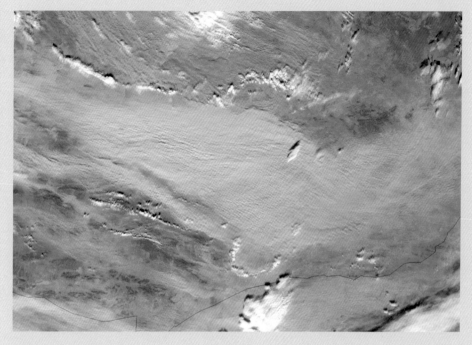

Figure 46. Loess deposits on the southern edge of China's Loess Plateau. This section shows several reddish-brown paleosols, each overlying a light coloured, loess deposit.

Figure 47. A large dust storm blows across 1,000 kilometres of the Gobi Desert in Mongolia in this satellite view taken in November 2002. The dust storm appears as a light tan area with blurred horizontal streaks against the darker desert. The Gobi Desert sits on a high plateau (from 900 to 1,500 metres elevation) and experiences extreme weather conditions, with bitterly cold winters and short hot summers. North is toward top of image.

hundreds of square kilometres in an area of north-central China known as the Loess Plateau, north of the Tibetan Plateau and the Himalayas. Here major rivers including the Yellow River have cut down through the loess, forming bluffs which stand over 300 metres high (Figure 45). Pinkish to red horizontal bands, representing old soils (paleosols) about one-half to several metres thick, alternate with buff colored loess bands, which are usually a little thicker than the paleosols (Figure 46). A complete section preserves a minimum of thirty-seven distinct red and buff couplets.

The couplets represent the stacking of loess beds, each with a soil developed in the upper part of the bed. Each loess bed and paleosol represents thousands of years of silt and fine sand deposition and soil development. The paleosols are similar to those developed today on the surface of much of the western Canadian plains and foothills. The types of soils vary depending on the physical and climatic characteristics of the environment. Some of the soils supported grasses, whereas others supported grasses and forest. The stacking of the paleosols and loess layers is a result of the accumulation and preservation of loess through time.

Loess can be suspended in the wind up to several kilometres above Earth and carried thousands of kilometres along the path of prevailing winds. The characteristics of the Chinese loess, such as grain size and mineralogy, indicate that the loess was blown into this area from the northwest and west, from the Gobi Desert (Figure 47) and from as far away as Afghanistan. We know that during cold and dry times the Siberian high pressure system, located just north of China, intensifies, producing winter monsoon winds that annually strike China. During and immediately after the winter monsoon period, windstorms carry huge amounts of dust. The winter monsoon appears to have dominated this area for thousands of years during a glacial period, accumulating thick loess deposits.

Once the winter monsoon begins to wane due to a milder climate, the moist summer monsoon system emanating from the south dominates. During warm interglacial periods less loess accumulates, or loess deposition may cease altogether. This is a time when warmer and moister conditions can initiate the chemical and physical processes that produce soils. Soil development depends on the time involved, the characteristics of the climate and vegetation, and the rate of loess accumulation. If little or no accumulation of loess takes place and enough time is allowed, well-developed soils can form, which explains the extraordinary alternating soils and loess beds seen in northern China.

Although winter and summer monsoons dominated over thousands of years, there were always seasonal variations between warm, wet and cold, dry periods just like there is today in eastern Asia. Figure 48B (page 38) shows the 37 alternating soils and loess units and the grain size variation in the Baoji section covering the past 2.6 million years. The relatively low rate of erosion makes north-central China one of the few locations in the world where such a complete record exists.

INTERPRETING

THE LAST ICE AGE

Putting it together— The last Ice Age

The oxygen isotope records from ocean and ice cores provide a big picture of global glaciations. $\delta^{18}O$ values show that about 2.6 million years ago Earth entered a time characterized by glacial-interglacial oscillations, collectively referred to as the last Ice Age. The swings in $\delta^{18}O$ values are used to define isotope stages. To keep track of these changes, $\delta^{18}O$ stages indicating cold periods are denoted by even numbers and warm periods by odd numbers (Figure 48A). The number 1 denotes our present climate as a warm period or interglacial. Over 100 isotope stages, indicating over 50 glacial-interglacial climate changes have occurred in the past 2.6 million years.

Figure 48. Two outstanding records of climate change that can be correlated for nearly all the Quaternary Period. (A) Oxygen isotope variation in a mid-latitude deep sea core from the North Atlantic Ocean equated to the marine oxygen isotope (MIS) stages. Age scale in millions of years. (B) Grain size variation in the climate-driven loess-paleosol sequence near Baoji, China shows a rough correspondence with the oxygen climate cycles. Vertical depth axis is non-uniform; it has been adjusted so that depths correlate with the age axis on the left side of the figure.

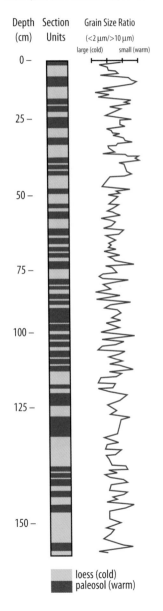

A. Deep-sea Core Record (DSDP Core 607)

B. Baoji Loess-Paleosol Sequence

The same conclusions can be reached with the loess-paleosol sequences (Figure 48B). The paleosols clearly identify warm, wet periods, while the loess units signify cold, dry periods. Grain size variation of the loess can also be used as a climate proxy. During cold periods higher wind velocities associated with the Siberian high pressure system and the winter monsoon enable coarser particles to be transported further south on the Loess Plateau. During summer monsoons winds are weaker and the grain size of the loess deposits decreases. These signals are remarkably consistent between the Pacific, Atlantic and Indian oceans. These results strongly imply that proxy climate data can be correlated and are indicating global changes in climate and in the amount of ice on Earth.

A time scale terminology has been created to describe this part of geologic time. In the last century there was a simple division: the current interglacial (isotope stage 1) that began 11,500 years ago was named the Holocene, and the earlier Ice Age cycles were placed in the Pleistocene. The Holocene and Pleistocene were grouped into the Quaternary Period. However the base of the Pleistocene is 1.8 million years old, whereas recent work shows the climate oscillations began earlier, in the late Pliocene about 2.6 million years ago. So, geologists have adopted the term Quaternary to encompass the time from about 2.6 million years ago (Figure 49). The term Quaternary makes sense as a time-stratigraphic unit and there is increasing support among geologists to extend the time of the Quaternary back to about 2.6 million years ago.

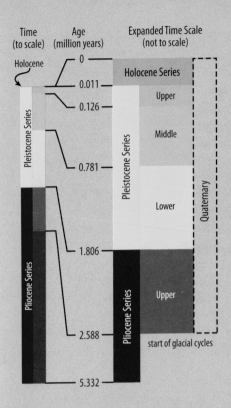

Figure 49. Time scale terminology for the Ice Age. The Quaternary is a time unit covering the oscillating glacial-interglacial extremes that began about 2.6 million years ago. The Holocene postglacial commenced at the end of the Younger Dryas cold period about 11,500 years ago. The Rocky Mountain glaciations discussed at length in this book are younger than 24,000 years and cover the Holocene and uppermost Pleistocene.

GLOBAL ICE

During the peaks of the glacial cycles there were two major ice sheets that covered large parts of the northern hemisphere (Figure 50). The largest was the Laurentide-Cordilleran ice sheet complex that covered most of Canada, Greenland, the northern United States and part of Alaska. Today, Greenland retains the second largest ice mass in the world, covering 6.7 million square kilometres with ice over 3,000 metres thick in places. The other large ice sheet was the Fennoscandian complex that covered most of northern Europe and reached into central Europe. Although ice sheets have been proposed for parts of northern Asia, most scientists have rejected this idea.

In the southern hemisphere the only wide-scale ice sheet occurred in Antarctica. It persists today, covering nearly 14 million square kilometres with a maximum thickness exceeding 5,000 metres.

Beside these large continental ice sheets, the lowering of the snowline during cold periods allowed glaciers to form and expand at higher altitudes, especially in mountainous regions such as the North American Cordillera, South American Andes, Asian Himalayas and Altai Mountains.

Figure 50. Global distribution of Pleistocene ice sheets. The major continental ice sheets of North America, Greenland and northern Europe were linked by floating ice shelves in the North Atlantic and Arctic oceans.

ICE SHEETS IN CANADA

The records from Greenland, Antarctica and the world oceans provide information on global change. However, for a large landmass such as North America, climate cannot be generalized.

Continental weather systems are influenced by both oceans—the Pacific air masses (notably those in the Gulf of Alaska for western Canada) and the regional heat transfer by warm Atlantic Ocean currents affecting the east coast

(see Figure 7, page 7). The interplay of temperature and moisture transport over the continent contributed to uneven timing of ice sheet growth and decay.

Of the two main ice sheets (Figure 51), the Laurentide Ice Sheet originated in three spreading centres located west, north and east of Hudson Bay and reached south into the United States and west to the edge of the Rockies. The Cordilleran Ice Sheet formed independently in the mountains of

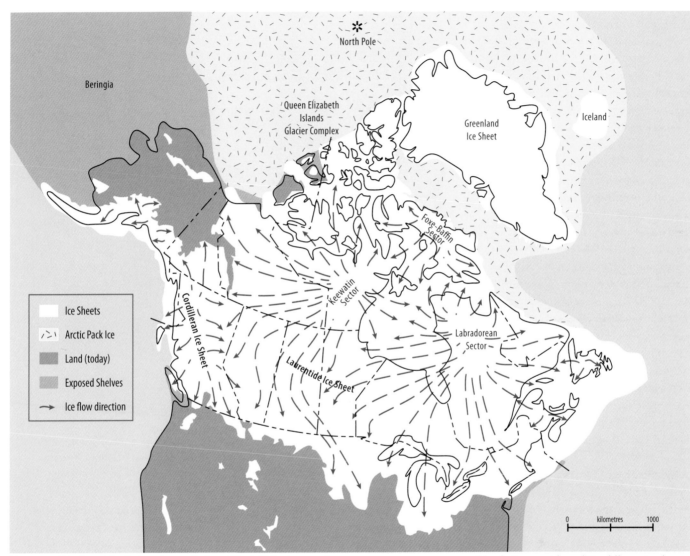

Figure 51. Northern North America at the Last Glacial Maximum, about 21,000 years ago, was covered by the Laurentide and Cordilleran ice sheets. The Laurentide ice spread from three centres around Hudson Bay—the Foxe-Baffin, Keewatin and Labradorean sectors. Cordilleran ice was confined largely to the western mountain region, although the two sheets met on the western Alberta plains. The Arctic Ocean was covered by pack ice. Sea-level lowering as a result of the ice buildup created a land bridge, called Beringia, joining Alaska and Siberia.

Alberta and British Columbia and was largely confined there by topography.

The physical evidence available to unravel the timings of ice sheet growth and decay decreases as we go back in time. Much of the evidence has been removed by younger ice sheets overriding and eroding the deposits of earlier glaciations. As field observations in different parts of Canada and the United States progressed, a general nomenclature for the last 240,000 years was developed (Figure 52). The Illinoian, 240,000 to 128,000 years ago, refers to a major, long-duration glaciation. This was followed by the Sangamonian interglacial, roughly 128,000 to 75,000 years ago, the Wisconsinan glacial from 75,000 to 11,500 years ago, and our current interglacial, the Holocene.

These events correspond broadly with the oxygen isotope stages defined from deep sea cores (which record global, not regional scale, changes). The irregular nature of the isotope curve within each stage indicates shorter term climate fluctuations. For example, stages 5b and 5d of the Eowisconsinan warm period are colder substages that may have been glacial in parts of North America, particularly around Hudson Bay. For this reason, the application of climate-stratigraphic names varies between Canada and the United States.

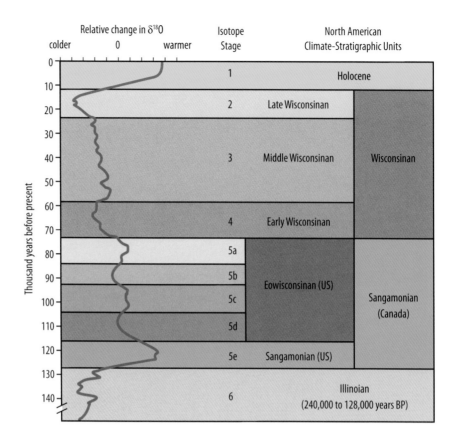

Figure 52. North American terminology of the most recent climate tied to global oxygen isotope stages. This diagram has been compiled from several sources and the age divisions (left scale) are generalized. Differences in terminology between Canada and the United States are noted.

For example, Canadians apply the term Sangamonian to the whole of isotope stage 5, whereas Americans restrict it to the distinctly interglacial stage 5e.

Stage 5e on a global basis is the Eemian interglacial, and was a distinctly warm period with temperatures as much as 5° C higher than today. Stages 5a to 5d, as mentioned above, were of intermediate character, with the exact climate probably location-specific. The early Wisconsinan glaciation, stage 4, primarily affected eastern Canada and the Baffin and

Hudson Bay lowlands, and may be related to changes in circulation in the North Atlantic Ocean. In the western Cordillera, the Early Wisconsinan was probably reflected as the expansion of alpine glaciers, rather than the formation of a massive ice sheet. During the Middle Wisconsinan interglacial, stage 3, a large area of western Canada was ice-free and the Cordilleran ice was probably restricted.

For the most recent glaciations of the Late Wisconsinan, stage 2, early expansion of the Laurentide ice sheet was fed by Pacific moisture moving across an ice-free Cordillera. As the Laurentide ice sheet expanded toward the mountains, it cooled the climate and prompted increased snowfall in the Cordillera that led to development of the Cordilleran ice sheet. Growth of the Cordilleran ice sheet, in turn, intercepted moisture that would normally have reached the plains. Thus the timing of the last glacial maximum (LGM) of the Laurentide ice sheet is somewhat earlier than that of the Cordilleran ice. The LGM of the Laurentide ice occurred about 26,000 years ago, whereas the Cordilleran ice reached its maximum around 18,000 years ago.

Cordilleran Glaciation

The rest of this book is concerned with the Cordilleran ice sheet in the Rocky Mountains. Nearly all of the evidence for glaciation in the Rockies relates to the last 26,000 years, covering isotope stages 2 and 1, the Late Wisconsinan and the Holocene, respectively. As the jagged oxygen isotope record of Figure 52 shows, there are smaller scale climate fluctuations within each isotope stage, and there is evidence in the Rockies for four late Pleistocene (Stage 2) ice advances and two within the Holocene (Stage 1).

Before discussing the glaciations, we must look at glacial processes and the evidence they leave behind.

FINDING

CLIMATE CHANGE IN THE ROCKIES

Climate records in the Rockies of Banff and Jasper National Parks are held in two geographic features: landforms and sediments. Climate history can be teased out of these deposits by application of geological principles and some of the climate proxies described in this book. A host of undisturbed landforms and sediments define the advances and maximum extent of relatively young glaciers (glacial periods) and the warming phases of deglaciation (interglacial periods). Although scarce, sediments indicating older glaciations and interglacials occur stacked in stratigraphic sections (see Figure 77, page 64).

A Complicated Record

When younger glaciers overrode the deposits of earlier glaciations, the older deposits were often eroded in whole or in part. This left a stratigraphic record containing information gaps due to missing sediments or depositional landforms. The biggest problem in reconstructing past climate from the Rocky Mountains landscape is the lack of complete stratigraphic sections. The records of climate change become more and more scarce as we go back in time. The Rockies do not possess the relatively complete records found in the Chinese loess, deep sea and ice core records. Geologists have been able to determine a relatively clear picture of the last major Rockies glaciation, but before that things become less definite.

Another complication is dating the climatic events. The relative ages of events are based upon the stratigraphic position of strata or landforms, younger on top of older. But sometimes landforms preserved on the surface are not related to each other. They may have been deposited at different times and represent different climate events. A moraine or glacial outwash deposit near Banff may look very much like another near Jasper. How do we tell if they are the same age or not? Absolute dating is the key, but there are few radiocarbon dates from the Canadian Rocky Mountains. The available dates show that the last major glaciation took place between about 10,000 and 25,000 years ago.

If only one glaciation occurred, working out the glacial history of the Rockies would be simple. However, we know that climate change has been responsible for a number of warmer and colder periods during the Quaternary. So where do we find evidence for multiple glaciation? Fortunately, not all evidence is lost through scouring by younger overriding glaciers or postglacial erosion. Even though landforms may be partially eroded, enough of a deposit may remain for scientists to reconstruct former climates. The trick is to match or correlate deposits that represent the same glacial or warm event. This may be difficult and without absolute dating control, may be impossible.

In mountain terrain, with its wide range of elevation, another factor has to be considered. This is elevation-induced regional climate caused by the decrease of temperature with altitude. While major climate events affect the entire globe, regional climates are superimposed locally on the overall change. Glaciers and frost features which might be considered a sign of overall cooling can occur in an overall warm period if they are at high altitude. These features can be seen in the Rockies today. The Columbia Icefield is a large ice mass covering more than 300 square kilometers, yet it is present in an interglacial warm period. As we reconstruct climate change, we must consider these aberrations.

The Rockies are part of a series of north-south trending mountain ranges along the west coast of North America that are collectively referred to as the North American Cordillera. The Rockies form the easternmost range of mountains in the Cordillera and were uplifted over a period of 40 million years to achieve their topography about 25 million years ago. Since that time the Rockies have been undergoing erosion by running water, chemical weathering and physical processes such as landslides. Rivers have cut v-shape valleys that drain onto the plains to the east and into the broad valley called the Rocky Mountain Trench to the west. For most of the 25 million years, the climate was warmer than that of today. It was not until about 2.6 million years ago that large-scale glaciation affected the mountains. Two million years is a brief period of time geologically, and even with large-scale glaciation the mountains have preserved their character. Nevertheless, glaciers have changed the valley profiles and left behind a variety of landforms and deposits.

BUILDING A GLACIAL LANDSCAPE

Before we interpret the evidence for past climate change based upon glacial landforms and sediments, we should briefly look at how today's alpine glaciation developed in the Canadian Rockies.

How a Glacier Flows

Glaciers form wherever the annual accumulation of winter snow exceeds the volume lost to summer melting over a period of many years. Snow layers change to ice as the snow crystals age and change shape and the older, lower layers are compacted by the weight of successively younger snowfalls. A glacier can be thought of as a river of ice. It behaves much like water, only in slow motion. Both water and ice respond to gravity by moving downhill, seeking the lowest elevation. Thus, when ice reaches a critical thickness, its weight will force it to flow laterally, spilling over the lowest point of any confining topography to flow downhill. It has two components of flow: one internal where the ice is deformed downstream and the other along its base where it moves over bedrock or debris beneath the glacier (Figure 53).

Ice movement in a glacier is not uniform. The most rapid movement is in the upper layers toward the centre of the glacier. The slowest movement is at the base and sides of the glacier, where friction with

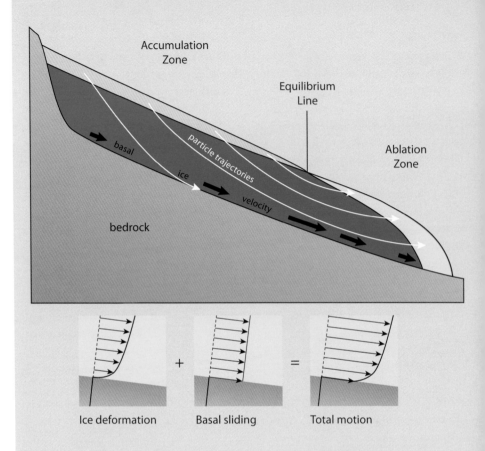

Figure 53. Dynamics of an alpine glacier. In the accumulation zone, precipitation exceeds melting and ice builds up. Driven by gravity, ice flows down to the ablation zone, where annual melting exceeds snowfall. The boundary between the two zones, where there is no net accumulation or wasting, is called the equilibrium line. Basal slip occurs at the bedrock-ice interface, and is highest at the equilibrium line. Rock fragments falling onto the ice surface from exposed bedrock are transported through the ice as shown by the white arrows. Inset diagrams below show how the total ice movement is comprised of internal deformation and basal sliding over bedrock or frozen sediment.

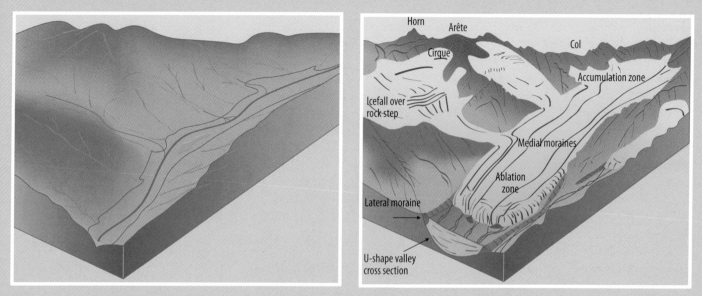

Figure 54 (left). Unglaciated mountain landscape. Valleys are sinuous and have a V-shape cross section.

Figure 55 (right). Glaciated mountain landscape. Ice and frost action sharpens mountain ridges by eroding glacial cirques. Arêtes (jagged knife-edge ridges) and cols (smooth divides) are formed by headward erosion of two opposing cirques. A sharp-pointed peak, called a horn, occurs where three or more cirques grow together. Valleys are widened, straightened and develop a U-shape cross section. Lateral moraines accumulate between the ice and the valley walls. Where two glaciers meet, the lateral moraines on the up-flow side are entrained in the resulting composite ice stream as medial moraines.

the confining rock surfaces slows it down. The shear forces created by the difference in velocity produces cracks in the ice, called crevasses, where the ice drags along sidewalls or spills over cliffs or rock steps in the bed profile (see Athabasca Glacier, Figure 127). If the ice is thick enough, a glacier whose terminus is retreating by ablation (melting and sublimation) still has an internal forward motion. Only when the terminus has thinned to a point

where glacial dynamics cease to respond will the terminus become stagnant.

Glaciers flow more rapidly in summer than winter, and may move from a few centimetres (typical movement) to over 100 metres (unusual surges) in a day. The overall velocity and distribution of velocity throughout a glacier depends on such things as the thickness, volume, density and temperature of the ice, and

the slope and bedrock nature of the confining valley.

High Altitude (Erosional) Features
Cirques (pronounced *sirks*) are concave depressions where ice first accumulates to form a glacier. Cirque development takes place where the elevation of the zone of maximum yearly freeze-thaw (the *snowline*) is more or less stable over many thousands of years. Yearly frost action

(freeze-thaw) with the proper drainage will form a depression called a nivation hollow. Eventually it will become deep enough to support perennial snow, and a cirque glacier develops. Cirque glaciers erode bedrock primarily by rotational basal slippage of the ice clogged with rock debris. This ice-rock admixture forms an abrasive surface which is able to erode the underlying bedrock, forming a half-bowl or amphitheatre.

The development of cirque glaciers is responsible for several other alpine features such as arêtes (jagged knife edge ridges produced by headward erosion), cols (smooth divides between two cirques) and horns (sharp-pointed peaks when three or more cirques erode back from different directions). An excellent example of a horn is Mt. Assiniboine, located just west of Banff National Park, even though the Matterhorn in the Alps is more famous. Cirques and related features are widespread in the Banff-Jasper area and can be seen in the mountains above about 2,200 metres.

Most likely today's glaciers did not form the cirques that they now occupy; they are just using cirques conveniently left by previous ice ages. Once the features are formed, succeeding glaciations alter the bedrock terrain very little. However, in the Banff area, commonly two cirques

at different elevations can be viewed in the same valley suggesting two different major climate events, where intense frost action took place over many thousands of years at two different elevations. A good example of a low level cirque, the C Level Cirque on the eastern flank of Cascade Mountain, can be visited by following a hiking trail from near Bankhead, on the Lake Minnewanka road near Banff. The cirque lies at 1,920 metres elevation and often contains snow in midsummer due to its shady east-facing aspect.

If the cirque glaciers expand beyond their cirques, they may become valley glaciers forming a fingering network. Where two glaciers meet, the amalgamation of their lateral moraines forms medial moraines in the combined ice flow downslope from their junction. Medial moraines are made up of ice with entrained rock debris derived from lateral moraines. It is common to view a series of parallel medial moraines in a major valley glacier indicating the coalescence of several tributary glaciers.

Rocky Mountain ice expanded out of the mountain front and coalesced with continental ice during at least one major glacial period (see section on Glaciation in the Banff and Jasper area). However, mountain ice was confined to valleys, and glacier movement was controlled by the

Figure 56. A U-shape valley cross-section is created by glacial erosion. This view is north up the Bow Valley from Lake Louise.

topography. We know this because we can identify the upper limits of glacial scouring on mountainsides, indicating that the ice did not overrun topography, and we find no glacial erratics (loose rocks derived from outside the area in which they originate) in the glacial deposits. In major valleys of the Banff-Jasper area the upper limit of glacial scouring is about 2,400 metres, whereas the major mountain peaks and ridges are at 2,700 to over 3,000 metres. A scour limit of 2,400 metres means that the glacial ice was about 1,200 metres thick. Although the vast majority of ice originated in cirques near the continental divide, glaciers must have crossed the low elevation Yellowhead Pass (1,200 metres) from the interior of British Columbia,

Figure 57. A prominent break-in-slope (arrow) above the town of Canmore marks the upper limit of the Canmore glacier.

Figure 58. Takakkaw Falls drops from a hanging valley into the Yoho Valley.

Figure 59. Striations cut into bedrock by moving ice. Coin provides scale.

because glacial erratics derived from the west are found in the Jasper area.

EROSION FEATURES

Unlike water, glacial ice exerts strong scouring action along its sides as well as its base due to the sandpaper-like qualities of large and small rock clasts caught up in the moving ice. This action modifies the valley cross section from V-shaped to U-shaped. U-shaped valleys are quite

common in the Rockies. Excellent examples are the Bow (Figure 56), North Saskatchewan, Athabasca and Spray River valleys.

Other erosion features associated with U-shaped valleys are breaks-in-slope that mark the upper limit of a glacial advance. They commonly form subdued longitudinal lines separating a lower slope angle above the line to a steeper slope angle below, because of differential

erosion. These are elusive and can be confused with bedrock structure, which may be in the same direction as the break-in-slope. However, careful examination and the detection of a slight slope down valley (the former slope of the glacier) can overcome this problem. An especially good place to view a break-in-slope is above the town of Canmore on the south side of the Bow Valley at an elevation of about 1,450 metres (Figure 57).

In addition to cirques and U-shaped valleys, glacier scouring also produces other erosion features. Hanging valleys occur where tributary glaciers fed into major valley glaciers. They did not cut as deeply as the major valley, and so were left hanging on the sides of the main valley when the ice melted. Today many are marked by waterfalls; Takakkaw Falls in Yoho National Park (Figure 58) is a classic example. Other good examples occur in the Valley of the Ten Peaks (Moraine Lake) and the Spray River Valley where it enters the Bow River Valley.

Roches moutonnées are ridges of bedrock that were formed by differential erosion at the base of an ice sheet. The term is derived from a French reference to wavy wigs of the 18th and 19th centuries that were held in place by mutton fat. Roches moutonnées are elongated parallel to the direction of ice movement, and rise smoothly on the side facing the ice advance. The lee side face is steep and irregular, reflecting plucking (quarrying) of bedrock by the ice. They are rare in the Rockies, but a good example can be seen near the terminus of the Athabasca Glacier. Look for a highly polished and striated, elongated bedrock mound about five metres long, tapering up valley but with a steep, rough, down valley face.

Striations are common features scratched into the bedrock by other rocks caught up in the flowing ice (Figure 59). Striations are commonly found in limestone bedrock surfaces, especially after they have recently been exposed by the removal of a protective cover like gravel or till. However, weathering of the bedrock after glaciation often removes striations quickly. Both roches moutonnées and striations can indicate the direction of ice movement.

Deposition Features

A glacier will continue to advance as long as there is enough ice being produced through snow transition to ice in the upper regions of the glacier. That is, the net gain of ice must exceed the net loss. Once ablation exceeds accumulation, the glacier will recede. Glacial sediments such as till will be deposited and a variety of glacial landforms such as drumlins and flutings, created during forward motion of the ice, will be exposed as the terminus of the glacier recedes.

Till

Till is probably the best indicator of glaciation. Till is an unsorted and unstratified deposit consisting of a wide range of grain sizes, from boulders to clay size particles, deposited directly from the glacier. Till usually is the principal ingredient of moraines. Several varieties of till are found throughout the Banff-Jasper area. They are based on unique characteristics produced by various dynamics of the glacier. One common variety is ablation till, which consists of debris on the surface or within the glacier that accumulates once the glacier recedes and stagnates.

Basal till is commonly found beneath ablation till. Usually the larger, relatively flat, rocks such as pebbles are oriented parallel to glacier flow. As the glacier ablates and there is little disturbance, basal till will retain the orientation of the pebbles. Basal till can be deposited while the glacier is moving or is stagnant. Material is picked up at the base of the glacier or is moved into basal position by a number of processes. One process is *regelation*, which is pressure melting at the base of the glacier, incorporation of rock debris from the bed load and refreezing down glacier. Also, ice flow paths within the ice sheet can bring material down to the base of the glacier. Good examples of basal till can be observed near the Banff Powerhouse section off the east side of the TransCanada Highway, near the Banff townsite turn off (Figure 70, see Road Log Stop 7).

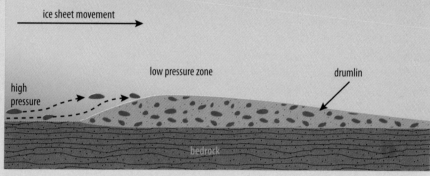

Figure 60. Upper: Drumlin well exposed on Morley Flats, seen looking north from the Trans-Canada Highway. Ice movement was from left to right; house on the right provides scale.

Lower: Mechanism of drumlin formation. Drumlin formation is triggered when ice encounters an obstacle as it flows over the bedrock. The obstruction creates a high pressure zone in the basal portion of the ice sheet. Bed load particles migrate from high to low pressure, and move up in the ice. When normal pressure is encountered, the clasts drop out, creating an accumulation of debris which thins downstream as the pressure is equalized within the ice sheet.

Drumlins and Flutings

Drumlins and flutings are streamlined landforms formed by forward motion of a glacier. Drumlins are tear-shaped features which taper in the direction of glacier flow. They are commonly a few hundred metres to over a kilometre long, a few metres to tens of metres wide, and a few metres to about 50 metres high (Figure 60). Flutings are usually longer, narrower and not as high as drumlins. The two features may grade into each other. They form in swarms and may cover many square kilometres in unconfined areas.

The origin of drumlins and flutings has been under discussion for over a century and there is still no consensus on their origin. Theories vary from depositional landforms caused by the accretion or plastering of material in layers at the base of the glacier while being subsequently molded into streamlined forms or caused entirely by glacial erosion and shaping of pre-existing deposits. Another idea is that they are formed by glacial melt water at the base of the glacier. Many flutings are eroded into bedrock. Drumlins are sometimes developed in bedrock but usually are composed of till, lake or river deposits. The answer to the origin probably lies in some combination of deposition and erosion. The streamlined slope is caused by glacial erosion. For this to happen, forward ice motion is necessary, even though a glacier may be retreating. This means that drumlins and flutings only indicate forward ice movement, not whether an ice sheet overall was advancing or receding.

Drumlinoid features are present in some of the major valleys of the Canadian Rockies such as the Bow, North Saskatchewan and Athabasca River valleys, and where they exit the mountains. In the Bow Valley, Morley Flats east of Kananaskis River is interrupted by many eastward trending drumlins composed of till. Several can be seen from the TransCanada Highway (Figure 60, see Road Log Stop 1). On the bordering valley uplands, drumlinoid features with the same general trend are eroded into bedrock. These features are best viewed on air photographs. Other examples of drumlins are in the Athabasca River Valley northeast of Jasper National Park, near Hinton. They form in swarms, some trending southward, having been formed when ice was deflected by the Laurentide ice sheet that flowed from the east. It is possible to view the interior of a drumlin in several locations along the logging road that runs northeast of Hinton (Figure 141, see Road Log Stop 32).

Figure 61. Lateral moraine on the south side of the Valley of the Ten Peaks at Moraine Lake, highlighted by early autumn snow. The Wenkchemna Glacier hugs the shaded base of the mountain. The centre of the valley is filled with probable landslide debris.

Lateral and End Moraines

Lateral moraines are composed of debris ground off the valley wall by the moving ice, and rockfall from the mountain slopes onto the surface of the glacier. This concentration of debris is stranded on the valley sides when a glacier melts, and marks the upper limit of an advance (Figure 61). End moraines occur at the front of a glacier, commonly displaying a cross-valley arcuate shape, where the terminus paused during a retreat. It is formed by material piling up in front of the moving ice. If a glacier retreats up-valley at a uniform pace, end moraines will not form. Rather, the valley will receive a uniform coating of debris.

Lateral and end moraines of early glaciations in the Canadian Rocky Mountains are scarce. Mass wasting, including avalanches, rock slides and frost action, has obliterated most traces of older lateral moraines from valley sides. Talus slopes and alluvial fans have also masked some of the evidence. However, in the Valley of the Ten Peaks there are distinct lateral moraines on the north and south sides of the valley at elevations of about 2,100 metres (Figure 74, see Road

Log Stop 13). There is a second but less distinct lateral moraine at about 2,300 metres on the north side. These form nearly continuous ridges that dip slightly down valley and can be easily seen from Moraine Lake. However, they are not easy to recognise once the valley joins the Bow Valley. Remnants of lateral moraines from this same glaciation are seen only rarely in other areas.

There is no area in the Canadian Rockies where clear-cut, distinct end moraines that are associated with a major glaciation can be viewed. They were either eroded by high energy streams or mass wasting down valley slopes, or they were never present due to dynamics of the glacier at the time. Perhaps the glaciers were never in equilibrium long enough to develop distinct end moraines.

However, the lack of end moraines is not the case with younger minor advances that developed in postglacial times (see section on Glacial History). Most cirque and valley glaciers in the Canadian Rockies today have well formed lateral and arcuate end (recessional) moraines near the terminus of the ice front. Many of these features are still ice-cored and will diminish in size as melting takes place (Figure 62). There may be more than one set of end moraines associated with a glacier but they are all associated

Figure 62. Athabasca Glacier moraines. The receding Athabasca Glacier (out of picture to right) left behind a small recessional moraine (foreground with person for scale) and a large sharp-crested lateral moraine (in middle distance, right centre of photo).

with young glacier advances that occurred after the last major glaciation. In other words, they indicate climate change over about the last 10,000 years only. They can be viewed at the head of cirques along the Icefields Highway (Crowfoot Glacier) and in the upper reaches of valleys near the Continental Divide (see Road Log Stop 16). The easiest places to view moraines

are near Mount Edith Cavell and the Athabasca Glacier in Jasper National Park, and Peyto Lake in Banff National Park (see Road Log Stops 17, 20 and 25). At the rapidly-receding Athabasca Glacier a series of discontinuous arcuate shaped end (recessional) moraines can be viewed between the highway and the present day ice terminus (see Road Log Stop 20, Figure 62). Their small size is a reflection of the amount of glacial debris incorporated in the ice at the time of melt-out.

Kames and Eskers

Ice contact sediments are stream deposits that are laid down in contact with retreating and stagnant ice, so they mark a warming trend. They are the result of high energy streams running on the surface, within and near the base of the glacier during the peak annual melting season. These streams pick up glacial debris and move it short distances during short periods of time. Kames are knobs and irregular mounds composed of steeply dipping, poorly to well sorted gravel and sand. Eskers form within or at the base of stagnant ice and mark the course of meltwater stream channels (Figure 63). When the ice finally melts the channels are let down onto the underlying bedrock or unconsolidated sediment, forming sinuous ridges composed of horizontally-bedded, poorly to well sorted, gravel and sand.

Figure 63. A meltwater channel flowing underneath glacial ice during summer melt carries debris from the bed load.

A large kame and esker complex is well exposed just outside the mountain front in the Bow Valley near the Kananaskis River. Kame mounds are about five metres high and esker ridges about six metres high (Figure 95; see Road Log Stops 2 and 3). The sediments in the kames are both poorly and well sorted, and dip steeply in a variety of directions. The eskers are composed of relatively flat lying gravels. This kame and esker complex is relatively intact, and must have been deposited during stagnation of the last glaciation that affected this area or else it would have been at least partially eroded.

The Emerson Lakes esker complex, located east of Hinton, consists of eskers that form steep sided ridges as much as 25 to 30 metres high (Figure 142; see Road Log Stop 33). These eskers were formed during the retreat of the last major glacier that flowed out of the Athabasca River Valley.

Ice-contact deposits are more elusive when the typical geomorphic forms have been eroded. Steeply dipping, poorly sorted gravels can be seen in exposures near Banff along the Cascade River, in bluffs near Canmore and around Jasper townsite. These deposits are remnants of ice contact sediments. Those in the Banff and Canmore areas were later overridden by ice during a readvance of the last major glaciation.

Many of the present day glaciers that are receding so rapidly have stagnant ice near their ice fronts. Glacial debris is slowly concentrating on the surface as well as material melting out from the bottom. The resulting deposits could form till, but glacial meltwater may erode much of the material, leaving only a few patches of till and perhaps a kame or esker. The Wenkchemna Glacier above Moraine Lake possesses a large area of stagnation. The Dome Glacier north of the Athabasca Glacier is essentially stagnant, since much of its ice supply from the Columbia Icefield is now cut off. The Athabasca Glacier, although receding, is still able to keep flowing right to its terminus because it has a better feed from the main body of the Columbia Icefield.

Outwash

Outwash deposited by glacial streams is probably the most widespread glacier deposit found in the Banff-Jasper region, no matter what the age of the deposit is. Outwash is composed mainly of flat-lying, moderately to well sorted gravel and sand. These deposits accumulate in front of the ice whether or not the glacier is receding or advancing. As the outwash is reworked by meltwater emanating from the glacier, it forms a braided network of interlocking channels and bars.

Figure 64. Outwash exposed on Carrot Creek, near Banff

Figure 66. Erratic boulder perched on a mountain side near Jasper

Outwash deposits deposited during the last major glaciation can be seen in outcrops in many exposures along the major highways in the Canadian Rockies. Near Banff and Canmore more than 40 metres have been exposed (Figure 64, see Road Log Stop 5). The best examples are along the river near the Athabasca Glacier, the braided network above Peyto Lake, and the upper part of the Bow, North Saskatchewan, Kicking Horse and Athabasca Rivers (See Road Log Stops 15 and 20).

Erratics

James Hector M.D., surgeon and geologist to the Palliser Expedition, in his report to the Geological Society of London on April 10, 1861 wrote: *Near the elbow of the North Saskatchewan a remarkable group of boulders of ... limestone, of enormous size, crosses the country in a line parallel with the côteau to the west. This line has been observed at points 30 and 40 miles apart. They occur as great angular masses, consisting of several beds of limestone, the coherence of which being very slight proves that they must have been stranded without any great violence. One of these masses contains over 3,000 cubic feet of stone, and rests on the plain obliquely with its south-western angle buried in the soil.*

These large blocks obviously made an impression on the observant Hector, in that they bore mention in his short 47-page paper covering no less than the geology of western North America from Lake Superior to the Pacific Ocean. Although he didn't realize it, Hector was describing a glacial erratic (Figure 65).

Glacial erratics are rocks which fall onto, or are picked up by, the advancing ice sheet and are transported long distances from their point of origin. They vary in size from pebbles and boulders derived from normal weathering to huge slabs deposited by landslides onto the glacier surface. When the ice sheet melts they are let down onto the land surface either directly (Figure 66), or via icebergs calved into adjacent ice-dammed lakes. Erratics are so-called because they are out-of-place in the host geologic terrane.

Figure 65. Hector's sketch of a glacial erratic on the plains of western Saskatchewan, 1861.

GLACIATION

IN THE BANFF-JASPER AREA

The various landscape and sedimentary features that we have found in the Canadian Rocky Mountains enable us to put together a picture of past glaciations in the Banff-Jasper area, although the record is fragmented and dating material is scarce. Using information derived from both inside and outside the Rockies, and placing our glacial events in the stratigraphic scheme used throughout North America, a sequence of six Late Wisconsinan and Holocene events emerges (Figure 67).

PRE-LATE WISCONSINAN GLACIATION

The earliest recorded ice advance in the Banff-Jasper area is inferred from outwash and a distinct "black" till underlying younger glacial deposits found in the Bow Valley and a few other localities in the southern Canadian Rocky Mountains. With the limited outcrops available, it is impossible to tell the extent or age of this advance. We can only say that it is pre-Late Wisconsinan.

LATE WISCONSINAN GLACIATION

The Late Wisconsinan glaciations began sometime after 29,000 years ago, peaked at about 20,000 years ago and receded to the higher part of the mountains by about 11,000 years ago.

The Bow Valley / Marlboro Advance

The most extensive glaciation for which we have clear-cut evidence is the Bow Valley advance. Glaciers filled the valleys in the Banff area and extended out through the Foothills into the Prairies, where they coalesced with the southwest-flowing Laurentide ice sheet. In the Jasper area, where the equivalent advance is called the Marlboro, the ice flowed down the Athabasca River Valley on to the Prairies where it also met the Laurentide ice sheet. Ice thickness reached about 500 metres, or to about

2,400 metres in elevation in the major valleys within the Front Ranges. At their maximum extent the glaciers formed a reticulated network, with the higher mountains and ranges above the level of the ice, not unlike the Columbia Icefield is today. A reconstruction of the glaciers in the Bow Valley might have looked something like the Arctic scene depicted in Figure 68.

The question is how do we know what the Bow Valley glaciation looked like? The evidence is fragmentary; all we can do is try to put the fragments together in order to get the best possible picture (Figure 69).

Probably the best evidence is the wide distribution of till found on valley sides and bottoms throughout the Banff-Jasper area. It is reasonable to conclude that this largely undisturbed till, with

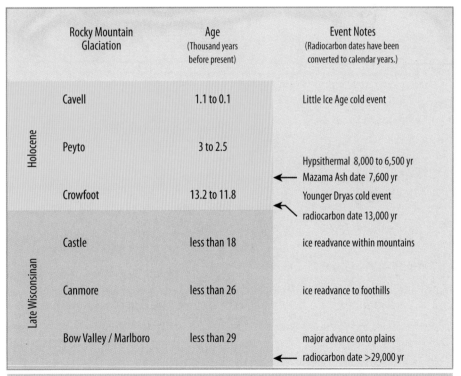

Rocky Mountain Glaciation	Age (Thousand years before present)	Event Notes (Radiocarbon dates have been converted to calendar years.)
Holocene		
Cavell	1.1 to 0.1	Little Ice Age cold event
Peyto	3 to 2.5	Hypsithermal 8,000 to 6,500 yr — Mazama Ash date 7,600 yr
Crowfoot	13.2 to 11.8	Younger Dryas cold event — radiocarbon date 13,000 yr
Late Wisconsinan		
Castle	less than 18	ice readvance within mountains
Canmore	less than 26	ice readvance to foothills
Bow Valley / Marlboro	less than 29	major advance onto plains — radiocarbon date >29,000 yr

Figure 67. Terminology and age of the Late Wisconsinan and Holocene glaciations in the Banff-Jasper area.

Figure 68. Modern glaciation of mountainous terrain on Ellesmere Island in the Canadian Arctic provides an analogy to the Wisconsinan glaciers in the Rockies. Amalgamated glaciers, where only the highest peaks protrude, feed a series of major valley glaciers draining to the ocean at bottom of the photo. This is comparable to the drainage of the Bow Valley glacier onto the Alberta plains. Compare with Figure 69.

similar characteristics everywhere, most likely was deposited by the latest, major advance. Otherwise the till would be largely eroded either by later ice, by streams or by mass wasting such as avalanching. As we shall see, this till has been run over by later, less extensive ice, but the ice didn't last long enough, or have enough erosive power to obliterate the evidence. Till deposits over 30 metres thick are exposed along the north side of the Bow River (Figure 70; see Road Log Stops 7 and 8) and on either side of the Cascade River east and northeast of Banff townsite. In the Jasper area good exposures are seen along the railroad tracks north of Jasper townsite and at the water supply site on the west side of the town (Figure 137; see Road Log Stop 26).

Other evidence for the Bow Valley/ Marlboro advance is drumlins found outside the mountain front along the Bow and Athabasca River Valleys. The orientation of the drumlins and the composition of the till tell us that glaciers that flowed out of these valleys must have formed the drumlins during the last major glaciation. In the Bow Valley area near Morley (Figure 71) the drumlins point toward Calgary. In the Athabasca River valley, the drumlins start out near Hinton aligned down-valley, but they change direction to the southeast (Figure 72). This change of direction

Figure 69. Conceptual view of the glacial ice fill during the maximum extent of the Bow Valley advance. The ice, shown in translucent blue, has been superimposed on a recent false-colour satellite view. High mountains appear magenta and lower elevations are brown. This was the most extensive Late Wisconsinan glaciation, with ice flowing out from the mountains onto Morley Flats. The Cordilleran ice limit has been mapped in the Bow Valley from Moraine Lake through to Morley Flats. However, the ice extent in tributary valleys and outlet valleys onto the plains is speculative. Ice from the Laurentide ice sheet occupied the plains well east of the mountain front.

Figure 70. Bow Valley till outcrop near the Banff Powerhouse along the Trans-Canada Highway. Sediment grain size varies from clay to boulders.

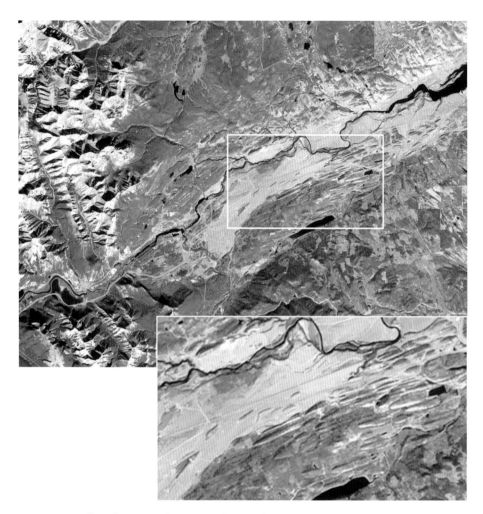

Figure 71. Satellite photograph showing the drumlin field on Morley Flats, created by ice flowing from the mountains during the Late Wisconsinan Bow Valley advance. Inset photo provides detail. Main photo covers a distance of 35 kilometres, from Lac des Arcs and the town of Exshaw (lower left) to the Ghost Reservoir (upper right). High mountains and the gravelly outwash plain of the Bow River appear magenta in this false-colour image.

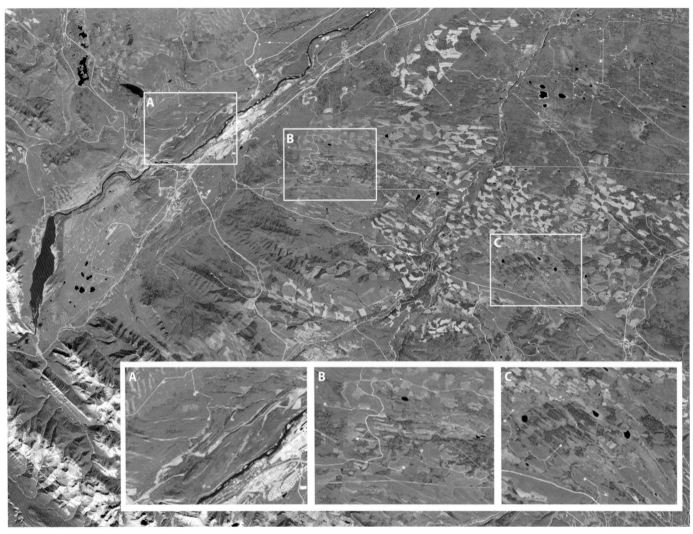

Figure 72. False-colour satellite photograph of drumlins shaped by ice emanating from the Athabasca Valley. The entrance to Jasper National Park is at the south end of Brûlé Lake (left) and the Athabasca River is prominent in the upper left of photo. From west to east (left to right) three highlighted rectangles and their enlarged images (bottom) show the change in drumlin orientation. At the town of Hinton (A), the trend is southwest-northeast, reflecting the flow of Cordilleran ice exiting the mountains. The drumlins are deflected as a result of encountering Laurentide ice, first in an east-west direction (B) then changing to northwest-southeast (C). Width of the main photo is approximately 60 kilometres.

Figure 73 (left). The Okotoks Erratic is derived from the Gog Formation in the mountains southwest of Jasper. Measuring 40 m long, 18 m wide and 9 m high, it weighs about 16,000 tonnes and is the largest rock in the Foothills Erratic Train (note people in the photograph for scale).

Figure 74 (right). Break-in-slope and lateral moraine (arrows) on the Mt. Temple massif on the northwest side of the Valley of the Ten Peaks at Moraine Lake. The lower arrow at about 2,100 metres elevation marks a forested lateral moraine left by the Castle Mountain advance. The upper arrow at the base of the empty cirque at 2,350 metres indicates a break-in-slope eroded by the older Bow Valley (Canmore?) advance.

records Cordilleran ice meeting with the Laurentide ice sheet and the amalgamated flow moving to the southeast. Marlboro till contains unique quartzite erratics that form part of the Foothills Erratics Train that runs along the east front of the Rocky Mountains into Montana. The Big Rock, found south of Calgary just off Highway 7 between Black Diamond and Okotoks, is part of this erratics train (Figure 73).

Other evidence for the Bow Valley advance are the breaks-in-slope as well as erratics that mark the upper limit of the ice. We assume that they were formed by the Bow Valley advance, the last major advance in the area. Breaks-in-slope can be seen at elevations of about 2,350 metres on the north wall of the Valley of the Ten Peaks (Figure 74) and at about 2,300 metres on the east side of the Baker Creek valley.

Some of the till deposits overlie thick outwash gravels that were most likely deposited by braided streams during the retreat of a previous advance that we know little about, or during the advance of the Bow Valley glacier. It is nearly impossible to say which interpretation is correct with the information we have.

We date the Bow Valley and Marlboro advances as Late Wisconsinan from a

Figure 75 (left). Carrot Creek, east of Banff town. Light coloured discontinuous till of the Canmore advance overlies darker outwash deposits left behind by the retreat of the Bow Valley glacier. The contact is near the top of the cliff.

Figure 76 (above). End view of a dissected esker on Morley Flats near Seebe. The esker is composed of gravel derived from the mountains to the west.

single radiocarbon date of about 29,000 years from twigs found below Marlboro till in the Jasper townsite area (see Road Log Stop 26) and dates on shells about 11,000 years old found in postglacial lake deposits near Pocahontas (see Road Log Stop 30) near the eastern gate of Jasper National Park. These dates bracket the age of the Late Wisconsinan glaciation in this area, although we need more dates to be sure.

Canmore Advance
The Bow Valley/Marlboro advance is well documented, but the two succeeding advances, the Canmore and Castle Mountain advances (described

below), are open to question. There is uncertainty whether or not they were distinct advances or part of the overall deglaciation of the Bow Valley/Marlboro advance without any succeeding advance phases. We favour distinct advances for the reasons that follow.

As the Bow Valley glacier receded up the Bow River Valley after its maximum extent, there are indications that the glacier readvanced from about the Banff townsite area to just east of the mountain front near the Kananaskis River. The readvance was probably short lived and the thickness of ice only about 230 metres near the town of Canmore. The evidence

for this readvance is pieced together from several lines of information.

The best evidence for this readvance is the presence of thin, discontinuous patches of till, similar to the till of the Bow Valley advance, located on the surface and overlying outwash deposits laid down during the deglaciation following the Bow Valley advance. These patches form drumlin-like structures and are found southeast of Banff townsite and in the vicinity of Canmore (Figure 75, see Road Log Stop 6).

Other evidence includes breaks-in-slope located along a discontinuous line on

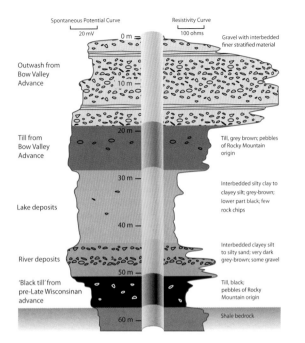

Spontaneous Potential Curve
20 mV

Resistivity Curve
100 ohms

0 m

10 m

20 m

30 m

40 m

50 m

60 m

Gravel with interbedded finer stratified material

Outwash from Bow Valley Advance

Till from Bow Valley Advance

Till, grey brown; pebbles of Rocky Mountain origin

Lake deposits

Interbedded silty clay to clayey silt; grey-brown; lower part black; few rock chips

River deposits

Interbedded clayey silt to silty sand; very dark grey-brown; some gravel

'Black till' from pre-Late Wisconsinan advance

Till, black; pebbles of Rocky Mountain origin

Shale bedrock

Figure 77. Electric well log from a borehole near Canmore, Alberta that provided clear evidence of multiple glaciations in the Bow Valley. Spontaneous potential and resistivity measurements taken in the borehole vary with the porosity in the different sediment types and the salinity of the fluids occupying the pore spaces. These measurements help to define the unit boundaries.

Immediately overlying bedrock is an undated pre-Wisconsinan till, informally designated the "black till." Overlying this unit is what appears to be river alluvium and a relatively thick unit of lake silt and clay. Near the top of the borehole is Bow Valley till, which underlies the uppermost unit of outwash gravels deposited by the retreat of the Bow Valley ice and predates the Canmore till. Patches of Canmore till lie above the Bow Valley outwash, but are not present at the borehole site.

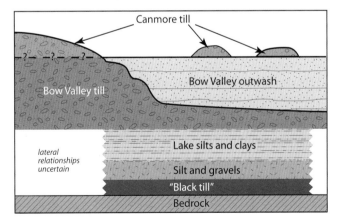

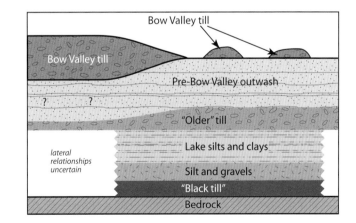

Figure 78. Sequence interpretation of the Canmore borehole. The left diagram is one author's (NR) interpretation, with patches of Canmore till overlying Bow Valley outwash and till units. An alternate interpretation in the right diagram assigns the surface tills to the Bow Valley advance, with pre-Bow Valley outwash and an older till beneath. This older till has not been observed in other areas.

the southwest side of the Bow River valley southeast of Banff townsite. Near the Banff National Park boundary, the breaks are at a maximum of 1,615 metres and near Canmore at a maximum of 1,555 m. This means that the ice sloped down valley at a grade typical for valley glaciers, forming a relatively thin tongue of ice that advanced from the Banff townsite area to beyond the Kananaskis River. Kames and eskers located in the plain between Kananaskis and Seebe formed during deglaciation following this advance (Figure 76, see Road Log Stops 1 and 3).

Another line of evidence for the re-advance includes ice-contact deposits near the confluence of the Bow and Cascade Rivers that laterally grade into outwash deposits down valley. These ice-contact deposits represent stagnant ice indicating a pause or an equilibrium phase before the Canmore re-advance.

The well log from a borehole drilled at Harvie Heights, near Canmore, supports this interpretation (Figure 77). The borehole passed through thick outwash deposits overlying till, both of which are interpreted as Bow Valley age. Patches of Canmore till appear at the surface near the borehole location.

The deposits associated with the Canmore advance could be interpreted other ways (Figure 78). One way is that the thin patches of till over outwash could be correlated with the thick units of Bow Valley till up valley. Therefore the underlying units of ice-contact and outwash deposits would be older than the Bow Valley till. If what we are interpreting as Bow Valley till is actually an older unit, then this alternate interpretation could be correct. However, we have never observed a similar till unit below Bow Valley till anywhere in the region, with the exception of the "black till" till mentioned earlier (Figure 77).

Evidence for a Canmore equivalent in the Jasper area remains elusive. However, near Obed along the Athabasca River there is what may be an arcuate shaped moraine representing a readvance of the Marlboro glacier.

Landscape morphology indicates that important drainage changes took place during the late phases of the Canmore advance. The present routes of the Bow River east of Exshaw and at the north end of the Kananaskis River are caused primarily by glacial deposits damming pre-existing channels. The flow of the Bow River around the south side of Tunnel Mountain and the present route of the Cascade River along the northeast side of the Cascade Valley result from the erosion of side and sub-glacial streams into bedrock during deglaciation. Finally, during the Canmore time and perhaps earlier, the major drainage of the area was through the valley of Lake Minnewanka, not along the Bow River Valley southeast of Banff townsite. The old course is evidenced by the east-facing wall of an abandoned waterfall (later artificially buried) at the southwest end of Lake Minnewanka, plus stream channel morphology and lower elevation at the east end of the valley.

Castle Mountain (Eisenhower) Advance

There is evidence for a final Late Wisconsinan readvance following extensive deglaciation of the Canmore advance. Glaciers readvanced from their cirques in the higher reaches of the Main Ranges down tributary valleys into the Bow River Valley. The Bow River glacier extended to about Castle Mountain Junction (Figure 79). (This event was originally named the Eisenhower Junction advance after a name prevailing at the time of geological mapping. However, the mountain named Mount Eisenhower later reverted back to its former name, Castle Mountain, changing the name of the nearby highway junction as well.)

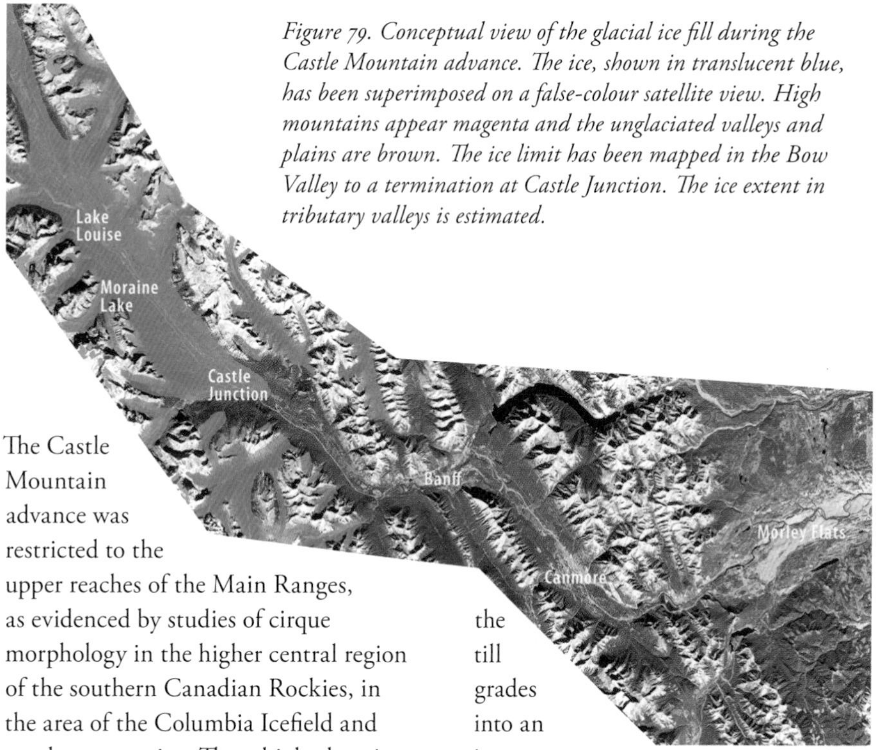

Figure 79. Conceptual view of the glacial ice fill during the Castle Mountain advance. The ice, shown in translucent blue, has been superimposed on a false-colour satellite view. High mountains appear magenta and the unglaciated valleys and plains are brown. The ice limit has been mapped in the Bow Valley to a termination at Castle Junction. The ice extent in tributary valleys is estimated.

The Castle Mountain advance was restricted to the upper reaches of the Main Ranges, as evidenced by studies of cirque morphology in the higher central region of the southern Canadian Rockies, in the area of the Columbia Icefield and nearby mountains. These high-elevation cirques that no longer contain ice are well developed, showing no signs of degradation. The fresh, unmodified appearance of deposits and cirques relative to older deposits suggest these features are younger than the Bow Valley or Canmore advances.

The best evidence for the Castle Mountain advance is ground moraine consisting mainly of till deposited in the lower parts of the Bow River Valley northwest of Castle Mountain. Near Castle Junction, the till grades into an ice-contact fluvial complex, in part representing the terminal moraine of the advance.

The ice was about 580 metres thick in the Bow Valley in the area of Panorama Ridge during its maximum extent. Most tributary valleys northeast of Castle Junction were occupied by glaciers and contributed ice to the major valley glacier, whereas certain cirques and glacial troughs in the vicinity of Castle Junction apparently supported glaciers at this time but did not contribute ice to the main valley glacier. Therefore, it is thought that the glacial complex formed a fingering pattern with disconnected ice bodies near the limits of the main activity.

The upper limits of the glaciers present during the Castle Mountain advance are well marked by fresh looking lateral moraines in Consolation Valley and the Valley of the Ten Peaks (maximum elevation 2,290 m), and by breaks-in-slope on the southwest side of the Bow River valley northwest of Castle Junction (maximum elevation about 2,060 m) (Figure 74, see Road Log Stop 13). Less convincing evidence includes breaks-in-slope at similar elevations in the Baker Creek Valley and the northeast side of the Bow River Valley southeast of Baker Creek. Also, there is a change in character of alluvial fans and the Bow River floodplain upstream from Castle Junction. These features are poorly developed compared to those down valley. In other words, the deposits and morphology appear relatively young when compared to older advances.

The interpretation of the Castle Mountain advance is subjective, and the evidence presented is not foolproof. However, we favour this interpretation until unequivocal evidence to the contrary is presented.

Holocene Ice History

As late Wisconsinan ice was waning in the Rocky Mountains, another short-term cold period was recorded widely in lands bordering the North Atlantic Ocean area by such things as vegetation changes and the formation of end moraines. This happened between 13,000 and 11,600 years ago and is called the *Younger Dryas* (Figure 80). This cold period appears to have affected more than the North Atlantic area. In the Canadian Rockies, the advance of the Crowfoot Glacier in Banff National Park is thought to be an expression of the Younger Dryas cooling (Figure 81, see Road Log Stop 16). Radiocarbon dates place the Crowfoot advance between about 13,200 and 11,800 years ago, so it was relatively short-lived. By 11,000 years ago the climate was back in a warming trend resulting in the recession of the mountain glaciers. The Crowfoot moraine system consists of arcuate end and lateral moraines that are seen in other areas of the Canadian Rocky Mountains where moraines have not been overridden by the late nineteenth century Little Ice Age moraines (discussed later).

Holocene climate and environment change are detected by studying features such as ice and rock glaciers, alluvial fans, talus slopes, moraines, volcanic ash, soils

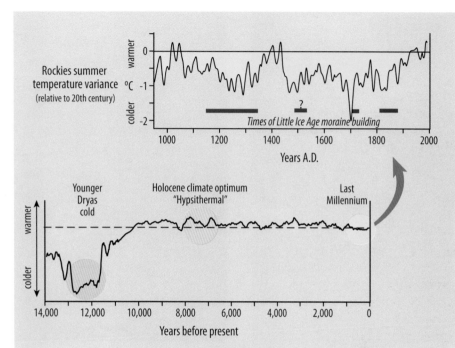

Figure 80. Holocene temperature record from a Greenland ice core showing the abrupt transition from the Younger Dryas cold 11,600 years ago to a warmer climate that reached an optimum about 6,500 to 8,000 years ago. The temperature record for the last millennium in the Rockies is shown in the expanded graph, based on work by Brian Luckman and others. Most Canadian Rockies glaciers reached their maximum extents in the mid-1800s.

and loess, and well-dated tree rings and pollen records from alpine lakes.

Changes in the type of vegetation largely correspond to change in elevation, and are divided into three zones: montane, subalpine and, at the highest elevations, the alpine vegetation zone (Figure 82).

The montane zone occurs mostly along major river valleys such as the Bow, North Saskatchewan and Athabasca. It has the most diverse vegetation, consisting of grassland and open woodlands. Trees such as lodgepole pine and aspen are found in the montane forests, along with Douglas fir on some of the dry rocky ridges and white spruce

Figure 81. *The Angel Glacier on Mt. Edith Cavell with lateral moraine from a Little Ice Age advance below.*

Alpine

Sub-Alpine

Montane

Figure 82. *Rockies vegetation zones. Athabasca River valley with Jasper townsite in the foreground.*

along streams and in other moist areas. It is intermittently snow-free in winter.

The subalpine zone occurs at higher elevation and experiences a harsher climate. Freezing temperatures can occur in all months and the frost-free period is brief, usually shorter than 30 days. Snowfall amounts are high. Closed forests of spruce, lodgepole pine and fir along with shrubs such as blueberry, green alder and prickly rose occur in the lower

subalpine zone. The upper subalpine zone contains similar tree species but in thinner forests that also include dwarf evergreen shrubs and heathers.

The alpine zone is the area above treeline and is characterized by bare rock, ice and snowfields, with some limited vegetation patches. Alpine plants generally hug the ground to capture heat and reduce moisture loss to wind. Heather and grouseberry give way to avens, moss

and lichens in the uppermost areas. Any tree species occur near the lower zone boundary. They are extremely stunted and may be twisted into a shrub-like growth form called *krummholz*, a German term meaning bent wood.

In the montane and subalpine zones fire has had a substantial effect on the type, variety and age of the vegetation. A clue to the past occurrence of fire is thick layers of charcoal seen in some of the exposed sediments of the area. An additional indication is even-aged stands of lodgepole pine that are most noticeable in montane environments. Climate change will cause alpine vegetation to migrate to lower elevations during a cooling trend or, conversely, migrate up slope during a trend to a warmer climate. The movement of vegetation is often expressed in terms of movement of the upper tree line, and can be detected by the presence of logs in cirque lakes or bogs above the present tree line, and by studying pollen assemblages in lakes or bogs.

The study of well-dated pollen assemblages has been one of the most prevalent methods of studying Holocene environmental change in the Rockies. After the Younger Dryas cold period, pollen assemblages suggest that a warm and dry period, known as the *Hypsithermal*, occurred about 6,500 to

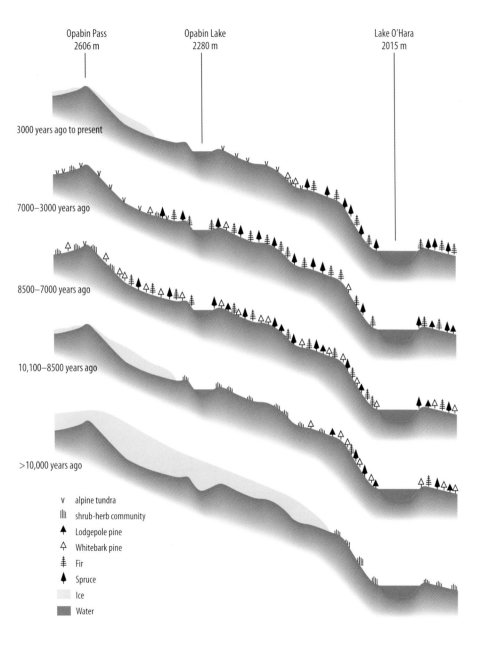

Opabin Pass
2606 m

Opabin Lake
2280 m

Lake O'Hara
2015 m

3000 years ago to present

7000–3000 years ago

8500–7000 years ago

10,100–8500 years ago

>10,000 years ago

v alpine tundra
�III shrub-herb community
▲ Lodgepole pine
△ Whitebark pine
‡ Fir
▲ Spruce
    Ice
    Water

8,000 years ago when mature forest cover migrated up-valley to formerly cooler areas (Figures 80 and 83). The drier climate also resulted in more frequent fires, indicated by an increase in charcoal layers. The Hypsithermal is followed by the *Neoglacial* phase. Treelines have been generally lower than, or similar to, those of the present during the Neoglacial, indicating a cooler climate. There is also evidence of glaciers advancing during the early Neoglacial from Boundary Glacier (near the Columbia Icefield), although this advance may be a local advance as opposed to a regional advance of glaciers throughout the Rockies. A more regional glacial advance, termed the Peyto advance, appears to have occurred about 3,000 years ago.

During the last 150 years glacier fronts have been generally receding from Little Ice Age maximum positions that were the most extensive in the last 10,000 years (Figure 84). As other Columbia Icefield glaciers have melted back in recent years, they have revealed fossil forests previously overridden by the ice. At the

Figure 83. Sequence of climate change in the Yoho National Park area determined by Mel Reasoner from pollen studies on sediment cores from Lake O'Hara. The tree line reached high altitude during the hypsithermal and retreated down slope with the onset of the Neoglacial (see text). Diagram after Reasoner, 1987.

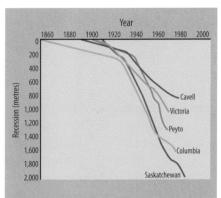

Figure 84. Recession of major Canadian Rockies glaciers in the last century. Measurement commenced with photographs near the start of the twentieth century and ended with the termination of the Water Survey of Canada glacier inventory in 1980. (Data compiled by Ommanney, 2002.)

Figure 85. Fossil forest exposed at the toe of the Saskatchewan Glacier after a storm attests to a glacial advance about 3,000 years ago that overrode and killed the mature trees.

Saskatchewan Glacier, the forest consists of subalpine fir, spruce and whitebark pine trees that grew about 3,000 years ago (Figure 85) but were killed and covered by ice in the Peyto glaciation. These trees were substantial, with individual ages of 225 to 262 years. The Saskatchewan Glacier must have terminated considerably up-valley of its present terminus for an extended period of time in order for a microclimate favourable to soil formation and colonization by vegetation to develop.

The Holocene climate trend in the Canadian Rockies appears to coincide with global climate trends. Pollen records from Europe show a warming trend during the early Holocene to a mid-Holocene maximum with a cooler and wetter climate thereafter, similar to the trends seen in the Rockies.

The "Little Ice Age" and Modern Glacial Records

Climate change in the Rockies is a very complex affair. Brian Luckman at the University of Western Ontario, together

with colleagues, has used measurements of tree ring latewood density and ring width to describe the summer temperature history of the Rockies during the last 1,000 years. The smoothed curve (Figure 80) shows the summer paleotemperature difference compared to the period 1901 to 1980. The past millennium was cooler except for brief periods in the early eleventh and early fifteenth centuries when the temperature was similar to modern time. The smoothed curve does not show the year-to-year variability, which ranges from +0.5

to -2°C. The only period of sustained cold summers occurred in the 1800s.

The *Little Ice Age* is a term used to describe glacier advances that occurred several times during the last millennium, between approximately 1150 and 1900 AD. The Little Ice Age was a time of fluctuating climate when glacier advances occurred in different parts of the world. In the Canadian Rockies many records document the advance and retreat of Little Ice Age glaciers. The records include well-developed end and lateral moraines near the termini of present cirque glaciers as well as end and lateral moraines in cirques where glaciers are totally absent today. These movements are dated by tree ring chronology, lichenometry and radiocarbon techniques.

Tree ring dating of moraines at the Peyto, Stutfield (a Columbia Icefield outlet glacier) and Robson glaciers suggests that advances commenced about 1200 AD to 1370 AD. Another advance may have occurred in the Rockies early in the 1500s. The most extensive glacial advances occurred in the early eighteenth century and during the mid to late nineteenth century. There are differences in the timing of glacial advances within the Rockies. At some northerly sites, including the Mt. Robson area, the eighteenth century advance was

Figure 86. Hilda rock glacier, viewed from the Banff-Jasper highway just north of Parker's Ridge and Hilda Creek.

Figure 87. Landslide from Mount Kitchener (out of view to right) just north of the Columbia Icefield is being cut through by the headwaters of the Sunwapta River .

slightly more extensive than that of the nineteenth century. In locations farther south, from the Columbia Icefield to Waterton, the nineteenth century advance dominates. The dated glacial advances correspond well with the cooler periods in the summer paleotemperature record.

POSTGLACIAL LANDSCAPE FEATURES

The present landscape in the Canadian Rockies is much like it was at the end of the Little Ice Age. Below are several postglacial landscape features that can be seen in many places throughout the Banff-Jasper area.

Rock Glaciers

A rock glacier is a stream of frost-shattered rocks that contains ice in the interstitial spaces. Expansion of the ice as it freezes reduces cohesiveness of the rock pile, and the rock glacier flows down slope under the influence of gravity, like a very slow ice glacier (Figure 86). One way a rock glacier may form is below rock cliffs that are fed by the fall of frost-shattered rock and avalanches. The rock insulates the interstitial ice and prevents the penetration of warm summer air. As a result, rock glaciers are advancing slowly or are inactive today, whereas ice glaciers are generally retreating. Most rock glaciers in the Rocky Mountains are

Figure 88. The town of Field, B.C. in Yoho National Park is built on an alluvial fan formed by drainage from Mt. Stephen.

at elevations of over 2,000 metres. The active Hilda rock glacier in northern Banff National Park (Figure 86, Road Log Stop 19) has advanced at an average of 1.6 centimetres per year for the past 200 years. The estimate is based on tree-ring chronology from wood buried near the front of the glacier. In spite of this seemingly slow rate, rock glaciers are an efficient means of transport, due to the volume of rock involved.

Landslides and Rockslides

Mass wasting refers to rock, soil and debris that have become unstable and move down slope under the influence of gravity. Rocks throughout the Rocky Mountains are relatively well fractured, and the expansion of water in the fractures upon freezing (about 10 per cent gain in volume from water to ice) helps to lengthen and widen the fractures and make the rock unstable. A well known example of a rockslide is the 1903 Frank Slide in the Crowsnest Pass of southwestern Alberta, where 30 million cubic metres of rock slid from Turtle Mountain in 90 seconds. Numerous other less spectacular slides can be seen along the roadside between Jasper and Banff (Figure 87, see Road Log Stops 21 and 22).

Alluvial Fans

An alluvial fan is a broad apron of poorly sorted coarse sand and gravel deposited by a stream where there is an abrupt lowering of its gradient, such as the change from a steep mountain slope to a flatter valley. The change in velocity of the water as it encounters a reduced gradient reduces its carrying power and causes it to drop much of its entrained sediment. As the name suggests, the sediment fans and thins outward. Recent alluvial fans in the Banff and Jasper area are widespread but are usually active only during the spring and early summer, when snow melt is the greatest. They commonly are responsible for eroding or masking older deposits. They form at the base of tributary valleys that flow into the major river systems, so many of the major highways cross alluvial fans. The north side of the town of Canmore and the town of Field, B.C. in Yoho National Park lie on alluvial fans (Figure 88). An outstanding example of an ancient fan can be seen at the Roche Miette Section (Figure 139, see Road Log Stop 29).

Figure 89. Talus fan on the south side of Moraine Lake.

Talus Slopes

Talus slopes represent a type of mass wasting. Talus consists of a loose collection of debris that forms when rock rolls down slope from bedrock cliffs due to the force of gravity. Talus slopes can be quite steep (25° to 40°) and form over long periods of time due to the slow erosion of rock from a cliff, commonly as a result of frost action. In rare occurrences, they may also form instantaneously after a landslide. Unlike alluvial fans, water is not involved in the movement of the material, although

water can certainly sort and redistribute material after deposition. Talus slopes are widespread throughout the Canadian Rockies. Outstanding examples are seen along the east side of Moraine Lake (Figure 89, see Road Log Stop 12).

Holocene Loess and Soil

In contrast to the outstanding records in China, loess and paleosols are rare in the Canadian Rocky Mountains. In fact, the only occurrences we have found are Holocene in age. Anything earlier was either eroded or never existed. In the Banff-Jasper area there are rare isolated loess deposits where they are protected from erosion, such as on the lee side of slopes. Generally, individual beds are less than one metre thick. Some of the best exposures consist of alternating paleosols within a series of loess beds. These indicate periods of loess deposition, followed by stability when the soil develops. Some outcrops contain bands of volcanic ash (see next section). The best exposures occur on the north side of the North Saskatchewan River where it is crossed by the Icefields Parkway (see Road Log Stop 18), and at the Roche Miette section off Highway 16 about five kilometres north of the Rocky River Bridge (see Road Log Stop 29).

Volcanic Ash

Volcanic ash in the Canadian Rockies is derived from active volcanoes in western Canada and northwestern United States. The ash from these areas consists largely of glass shards rich in silica that are transported in the direction of the prevailing wind. If the ash is dated, for example, by fission track dating of the shards or radiocarbon dating of plant debris, then the ash can be used as a time line to aid in the reconstruction of Earth history. Volcanic ash is easily eroded on land, so ash in the Rockies is commonly found in lake sediments, floodplain deposits or in loess sequences, where the loess has been deposited over the volcanic ash before it could be eroded away. So far, all volcanic ash layers found in the Banff-Jasper area are of Holocene age.

Dating of Holocene events in the Banff and Jasper areas is helped by the presence of three distinct and widespread volcanic ashes (Figure 90). The Mazama ash is generally the thickest and most widespread. It was deposited following the eruption of Mount Mazama in southern Oregon (now the site of Crater Lake), about 7,600 calendar years ago. It has been identified throughout the Banff-Jasper area and is found as far east as Saskatchewan and north past Edmonton. There may have been more than one Mazama eruption, as suggested

by mineralogical variations between the Mazama ash layers deposited at slightly different times. At some exposures in the mountains it reaches thicknesses of about six centimetres and is usually seen as a light grey band within Holocene sequences (Figure 91, see Road Log Stops 18 and 19).

Mount St. Helens in Washington produced numerous ashes during the Holocene. Over the interval about 4,000 to 3,000 years ago, the volcano produced more than a dozen discrete layers near its vent. One particular ash, the St. Helens Yn, formed a narrow plume extending northeastward into Canada. Its age is about 3,600 years. There is a debate about an earlier St. Helens ash found at Pocahontas and Brûlé Lake near Jasper and at Kootenay Plains on the North Saskatchewan River east of the Saskatchewan River Crossing. It is dated at about 4,850 years (see Road Log Stop

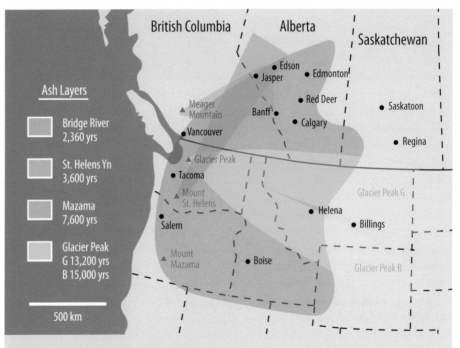

Figure 90. Ash distribution and dates for several eruptions along the Pacific coast ranges. Ages shown are approximate calendar years before present.

The Mazama and Bridge River ashes are both present in the section at the North Saskatchewan River Crossing (see Road Log Stop 18), whereas the St. Helens Yn is exposed at the Pocahontas Ash Site (see Road Log Stop 30).

A further ash derived from Glacier Peak, Washington, has been recognized from sites east of the Rockies in southern Alberta but has not yet been firmly identified from within the mountains. It has been assigned a tentative age of about 13,200 calendar years and correlated with Glacier Peak G ash found in Montana and Manyberries, Alberta.

Figure 91. Mazama Ash forms a prominent light band (middle of photo) in outcrops near the North Saskatchewan River Crossing. Coin at the base of the ash (arrow) provides scale.

30) and has some characteristics similar to the Yn ash. So do we have two Yn ashes deposited at different times?

Another ash, the Bridge River, originated from the vicinity of Mount Meager, near Lillooet, B.C. and is widely distributed throughout northern Banff and southern Jasper National Parks. It is dated about 2,360 years.

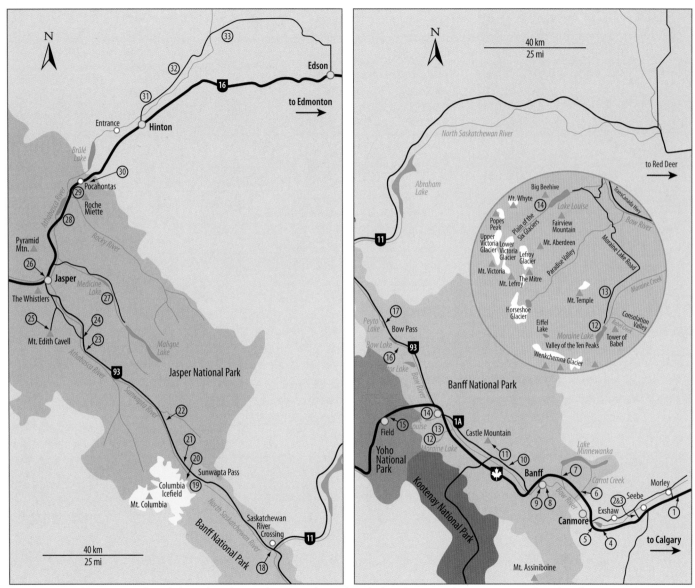

Figure 92. Road log maps with circled numbers showing locations of stops described in the text. Left: Jasper National Park and Hinton-Edson area. Right: Banff National Park and vicinity. Inset shows Lake Louise-Moraine Lake area in greater detail. Coordinates available on page 119.

ROAD LOG

GUIDE TO LANDSCAPE FEATURES

This chapter describes several landscape features that are easily accessible from the major highways and roads in Banff and Jasper National Parks. Most are indicative of past climate change indicating pre-glacial, glacial, and post glacial environments. The locations are on the accompanying maps (Figure 92) and some illustrations from earlier chapters are repeated here for easy reference.

Morley Flats and Canmore Area

Stop 1: Drumlins, Morley Flats

This stop is at the eastern end of the drumlin field on Morley Flats, along the TransCanada Highway (Figure 93). The drumlins were most likely formed during the advance of the Late Wisconsinan Bow Valley glacier that flowed well beyond the Foothills. They consist of Bow Valley till in contact with the underlying Mesozoic shale. The till consists of rounded limestone and quartzite pebbles and boulders together with shale and coal fragments from the bedrock set in a matrix of finer sand, clay and silt. Individual drumlins are up to a kilometre in length and they either stand alone or interfere with each other to form larger complexes. After the ice retreated, meltwater flowing down the Bow and Kananaskis valleys modified the shape of drumlins in the central part of Morley Flats and surrounded them with outwash gravels (see Stop 5).

Stop 2: Esker, Morley Flats

Highway 1X is a short stretch of road that joins the TransCanada Highway with Highway 1A at Seebe. It traverses a region of stagnant ice features, including kames and eskers, that is bordered by outwash gravels. These deposits extend eastward from the mountain front to just beyond the Kananaskis River. At this stop, a cross section of a dissected esker can be seen a few hundred feet from the southwest side of the road (Figure 94). Its poorly sorted gravels consist mostly of limestone, dolomite and quartzitic sandstone derived from mountains to the west. The stagnant ice features were probably deposited during the retreat of the ice of the Canmore advance.

Figure 94. Esker adjacent to Highway 1X.

Figure 93. Satellite view of the drumlin field at Morley Flats. For a larger view that puts this area in context, see Figure 71, page 60. The drumlins that have been modified by meltwater flow are surrounded by outwash gravels that appear pink. Intact drumlins appear in the green area south of the Bow River. Inset: Individual drumlin at the east end of the drumlin field. For larger photo see Figure 60, page 51.

Stop 3: Kame, Morley Flats

Northeast of the road the hummocky terrain represents kames associated with the region of stagnant ice features described above. They consist of steeply dipping, poorly sorted gravels (Figure 95). Unfortunately, exposures of the kame deposits can no longer be viewed due to site reclamation work.

Figure 95. Kame deposit on Morley Flats.

Figure 96. Sand bluffs bordering Lac des Arcs.

Figure 97. Glacial outwash exposed west of Exshaw.

Stop 4: Sand Bluffs, Lac des Arcs

Sand bluffs border Lac des Arcs and can be seen on the south shore near the campground boundary (Figure 96). They are composed of calcareous, well sorted, laminated to thinly laminated silty sand, with occasional cross-bedding, and contain fossil snails, wood fragments and clay-sized material. These sediments were deposited in Lac des Arcs during deglaciation following the Canmore advance, when water levels were higher than at present. Since that time, bluffs have formed by winds reworking much of the original material.

Stop 5: Outwash

Thick beds of glacial outwash were deposited during the retreat that followed the Bow Valley advance. The outwash was probably laid down when the retreating ice front was about six kilometres to the northwest of Canmore, deposited as a braided stream extending across the Bow Valley. Down valley, the material becomes better sorted and less coarse grained, and the direction and steepness of the beds become less varied. The outwash has subsequently been partly eroded and now forms a terrace that is being quarried (Figure 97). The gravel consists mainly of subrounded pebbles of limestone, dolomite, quartzitic sandstone and chert. Cross-bedding is common.

BANFF AREA

STOP 6: CARROT CREEK SECTION

Carrot Creek is accessible from the TransCanada Highway south of Banff. Poorly sorted outwash is exposed along the north side of the creek. Deposition of the outwash by braided streams took place during the ice retreat following the Bow Valley advance. Overlying the outwash are discontinuous patches of Canmore till that record the subsequent advance of Canmore ice (Figure 98).

STOP 7: POWERHOUSE SECTION

On the northeast side of the road are vertical cliffs of till typical of that found in the Bow Valley. The greater portion of this till was laid down at the time of the Bow Valley advance. However, the Canmore advance probably originated from this area, and the upper part of the till is therefore equated with this event.

Bow Valley till is composed mainly of calcareous sand, silt and clay plus approximately 20 per cent gravel. The gravel is dispersed in the finer sediment and sometimes forms lenses (Figure 99). Many of the stones display striated surfaces and the deposit has a weak fabric in which the long axes of the particles lie approximately parallel to the direction of glacier movement. These characteristics suggest that Bow Valley till is mostly a basal till. Dolomite and limestone predominate, with lesser amounts of quartzitic sandstone, quartzite, chert, shale, and pebble conglomerate. Pebbles of altered basic igneous rock are found occasionally and are probably from the Crowfoot Dyke, an magma intrusion

Figure 98. Carrot Creek shows good exposures of bedded outwash deposits. The uppermost part of the outcrop consists of discontinuous patches of lighter coloured Canmore Till.

Figure 99. Gravel lens within the Bow Valley till.

STOP 8: HOODOOS, TUNNEL MOUNTAIN VIEWPOINT

The Hoodoos Viewpoint is located opposite the campground on Tunnel Mountain Drive. Prominent hoodoos, or resistant pillars, can be seen (Figure 100) down the steep slope toward the Bow River. The upper part of these pillars is composed of Bow Valley till whereas the lower part consists of outwash gravels. This is the same till sequence that was seen at the Powerhouse (Stop 7) about 1.5 kilometres to the north. Differential weathering and erosion, controlled mainly by the strength of reprecipitated calcium carbonate cement, account for the resistant pillars standing out, while the surrounding relatively poorly cemented sediment was washed away.

In the area of Hoodoos Viewpoint road and at the Banff exit from the TransCanada Highway, post-glacial loess and wind-blown sand are present at the surface. A bed of Mazama ash about 7,600 years old is exposed in a road cut at the Banff exit.

STOP 9: BOW FALLS

The area around Bow Falls is one of the few places in Banff National Park where a stretch of the Bow River channel is cut into bedrock (Figure 101). The incision

Figure 100. Hoodoos seen from the Tunnel Mountain viewpoint.

that cuts across the Bow Valley near Bow Lake, 90 kilometres to the northwest.

Laboratory study of the till reveals no material that could not have been derived within the Bow River drainage area. The absence of distinctive rock types such as granite, that occur within 65 kilometres southwest of the Continental Divide, indicates there was little or no movement of ice from that area. Therefore, glaciers that extended into the Banff area must have originated within the Rocky Mountains.

Figure 101. Bow Falls

resulted from the diversion of the river from its earlier, well-developed floodplain when its natural drainage through Lake Minnewanka was dammed by glacial ice or sediment during the Canmore advance. The gap between Mount Rundle and Tunnel Mountain was probably originally eroded by a side glacier or subglacial stream. The width and polishing of the gap suggest that readvancing ice may have flowed though it. Later, it was occupied by the present Bow River.

but it has been modified by glaciation. It forms a hanging valley above the Bow Valley. Rockbound Lake occurs in a bowl-shaped depression within the cirque at an altitude of about 2,250 metres (Figure 103). Other cirques not visible from the highway are well developed on the northeast side of the massif. It is believed that the maximum thickness of ice extended up the mountain no higher than about 2,400 metres, although not clearly indicated.

Figure 102. The ramparts of Castle Mountain seen from the Bow Valley.

STOP 10: HIGHWAY 1A SLUMP

From this stop onward for about three kilometres, the road passes through post-glacial slump deposits. Rubble and slump blocks cover an area of about four square kilometres, forming irregular mounds and depressions similar to knob and kettle topography typical of glaciated regions. The slumped rock consists mostly of Mesozoic sandstone and shale.

STOP 11: CASTLE MOUNTAIN LOOKOUT

To the northeast are the post-glacial slump deposits seen at Stop 10. To the northwest, Castle Mountain rises to an elevation of over 2,800 metres (Figure 102). The wide valley behind the cliffs, visible from the highway to the south, was created by mountain structure,

Figure 103. Rockbound Lake occupies a former cirque behind the cliffs of Castle Mountain.

MORAINE LAKE

STOP 12: MORAINE LAKE

Moraine Lake exists because of a natural dam located at a narrow point in the Valley of the Ten Peaks (Figure 104). The dam probably consists of landslide debris from the slopes of Mount Babel to the southeast. However, because its composite conical shape is not typical of a landslide deposit, it is possible that the material was deposited on a glacier and, with the melting of the ice, developed the present morphology. If such were the case, the deposit would be called a moraine.

Figure 104. Landslide deposit blocks the Ten Peaks valley, creating Moraine Lake.

Good examples of talus slopes and alpine glacial morphology can be seen on the east side of the lake (Figure 105) from the lakeshore or, better yet, from the short trail leading to a viewpoint on top of the dam deposit. From the viewpoint, the forested lateral moraine from the Castle

Mountain advance is evident on the northwest side of the valley (Figure 74, page 62).

Moraine Lake is fed by the shrinking Wenkchemna Glacier. The glacier is seen best from the hiking trail that runs along the north side of the valley toward Eiffel Lake. Although it is nearly four square kilometres in area, the two-thirds of the ice in the central part of the valley is covered by rock fragments,

giving the Wenkchemna Glacier a deceptive appearance. At its terminus the Wenkchemna Glacier is bordered by ice-cored moraine that probably formed during the Little Ice Age (Figure 106).

The Wenkchemna Glacier is nearly inactive. However, Moraine Lake receives enough silt and clay from meltwater to create the characteristic turquoise colour of glacially-fed mountain lakes. Clay and silt size particles, or *rock flour*, derived

Figure 105. Moraine Lake and the Valley of the Ten Peaks. Massive talus fans descend to the lakeshore, while chaotic deposits from the Wenkchemna Glacier are seen in the distance.

Figure 106. Sharp-crested neoglacial lateral moraine and chaotic ice-cored deposits at the head of Moraine Lake are associated with the Wenkchemna Glacier.

from ice grinding against the bedrock are transported by glacial meltwater and remain in suspension when they enter the lake. The incoming rock flour can be observed easily at the head of Lake Louise (Figure 113) and at Peyto Lake (Figure 118). The particles break up sunlight into its component wavelengths. The longer wavelengths, reds and yellows, are absorbed by the water, whereas the shorter wavelengths, blues and greens, are returned to the surface, giving the water its characteristic turquoise colour.

STOP 13: MORAINE LAKE ROAD

To the southwest, above the road, a prominent lateral moraine rises to about the upper limit of thick forest vegetation. This moraine was formed during the Castle Mountain advance, at which time

Figure 107. View from the Moraine Lake road, looking south. Medial moraine from the Castle Mountain advance extends as a forested ridge (arrow) down-valley from the Tower of Babel (centre). Consolation Valley (left) and Valley of the Ten Peaks (right).

the ice reached a maximum elevation of approximately 2,100 metres. Although the upper limit of this moraine is obscured, the corresponding moraine on the southeast side of the valley extends about two-thirds the distance up the mountainside.

A remnant of a medial moraine extends from the flat topped, bedrock pillar known as the Tower of Babel (Figure 107). During the Castle Mountain advance this medial moraine separated the ice stream that flowed from the Consolation Valley, east of the Tower of Babel, from the main ice stream that flowed from the Valley of the Ten Peaks. The ridge seems too large to be entirely composed of medial moraine. There is probably an underlying geologic structure component, with bedrock lying close to the surface along the trace of the moraine.

Lake Louise

STOP 14: LAKE LOUISE

Lake Louise probably results from damming by a recessional moraine that extends from the mountain on the north side of the lake and continues, behind Chateau Lake Louise, to the base of Fairview Mountain on the south side (Figure 108). The age of the moraine is unknown. Well-developed talus slopes have formed at the base of the enclosing mountains.

The Victoria Glacier forms the backdrop to the view toward the head of the lake (Figure 109). A much better appreciation of the glacial landscape can be obtained from the Plain of Six Glaciers trail that starts along the west side of the lake and climbs to a lookout point 6.6 kilometres away. The Victoria Glacier is a continuous ice stream that descends from Abbot Pass (2,923 metres, not visible from the east end of the lake) into the broad valley (Figure 110). However, it is fed mainly

Figure 108 (top). Lake Louise is dammed behind a forested recessional moraine passing behind the hotel and continuing to the slope of Fairview Mountain (upper right in photo).

Figure 109 (bottom). The Victoria Glacier feeds Lake Louise.

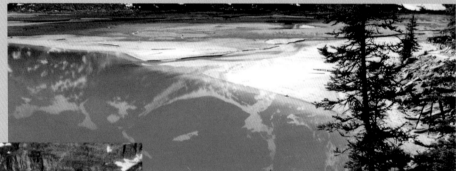

Figure 110 (top left). The Victoria Glacier descends from Abbot Pass at 2,923 metres elevation.

Figure 111 (top right). Ice and snow avalanches from high on Mt. Victoria feed the lower reach of the glacier. Note the annual banding in the ice cliff face.

Figure 112 (lower left). The lower part of the Victoria Glacier is heavily covered by rock debris. A sharp-crested moraine in right centre of photo marks where a now-vanished glacier descended from the northeast (right) to merge with the Victoria Glacier.

Figure 113 (lower right). Rock flour derived from glacial erosion enters the head of Lake Louise. Fine silt and clay held in suspension gives the lake its characteristic turquoise colour.

by snow and ice avalanches from the hanging glacier 300 metres above on Mount Victoria (Figure 111). The lower quarter of the glacier is covered by rock debris (ice-cored moraine), making the terminus appear indistinct (Figure 112). Downstream ice movement on the upper reaches of the Victoria Glacier is about 30 metres per year, but melting has caused the terminus to recede about 13 metres per year in recent times. Tributary glaciers, such as the Lefroy Glacier, have separated from the Victoria Glacier (Figure 114) in recent decades. Part of the Six Glaciers trail passes beside a vegetation-free, knife-edge ridge of fresh looking debris that is, in part, an ice-cored lateral moraine deposited during a Little Ice Age advance (Figure 112).

Figure 114. The Lefroy Glacier flows north from the headwall of The Mitre (background) and Mount Lefroy (hidden in the right distance). It used to merge with the Victoria Glacier on the Plain of Six Glaciers. This 1988 photo shows it has receded up-valley and has separated from the Victoria Glacier.

FIELD TO SASKATCHEWAN CROSSING

STOP 15: KICKING HORSE RIVER

The Kicking Horse River is an outstanding example of a glacially-fed braided river. When high energy meltwater runoff from mountain slopes reaches the lower gradient of the Kicking Horse Pass, the flow velocity decreases and coarser sediment is deposited on the flats around Field, British Columbia. The river splits into multiple shifting channels as the water courses around the deposited bed load. Runoff is greatest during the peak melting months of July and August (Figure 115). During most of the year low flow occurs and only a few channels are occupied by low energy streams (Figure 115 inset). At these times, one can see the riverbed and thousands of stranded tree trunks and appreciate the power of the water in moving coarse sediment and debris during the peak season.

Notice the large drainage chute coming down the eastern flank of Cathedral Mountain on the south side of the valley Figure 116). High on the mountain lies a small lake, dammed by the Cathedral Glacier. The ice dam fails periodically, sending water and rock debris downslope to cover the railway and even the highway across the valley. Following repeat occurrences, the chute was built to

Figure 115. The Kicking Horse River, just east of Field, B.C., seen in mid-summer. High-energy glacial meltwater continually modifies the braided channels. After the summer melt ends, the river flow declines greatly, as shown in the inset photo taken in October.

Figure 116. The man-made chute controls debris flows from high on Cathedral Mountain.

deflect the flow of debris along one path, protecting the transportation corridor.

STOP 16: CROWFOOT GLACIER

The Crowfoot Glacier and moraine are clearly seen at this site (Figure 117). The Crowfoot moraine has been overridden by a Little Ice Age advance during the last century. The Crowfoot moraine commonly displays a more subdued morphology, more vegetation cover, and deeper soil development than the adjacent moraines. Mazama ash (7,600 years old) is present in soils covering the Crowfoot moraine and, until recently, was the only chronological constraint for the timing of the Crowfoot advance.

The modern Crowfoot Glacier terminates in an icefall at the top of the cliffs above the Little Ice Age and Crowfoot moraines, and is about 1.5 square kilometres in area. Photographs from ca. 1920 show the Crowfoot Glacier extending to the valley floor. The Little Ice Age moraines are the sharp-crested, unvegetated ridges that are visible just above the forest. The boulder covered, forested ridge bordering the western shore of Crowfoot Lake is the Crowfoot moraine.

A suite of sediment core samples was recovered from Crowfoot and Bow lakes, which lie adjacent to the Crowfoot

Figure 117. Crowfoot Glacier with a prominent Little Ice Age moraine in the foreground.

moraine. The core samples help to identify and date sediments related to the Crowfoot advance. Age dates between 13,200 and 11,800 years indicate that the Crowfoot advance is approximately synchronous with the European Younger Dryas cold event. These findings illustrate that the climatic change responsible for the Younger Dryas event was not restricted to the northern Atlantic basin and Western Europe.

STOP 17: PEYTO GLACIER AND PEYTO LAKE

Peyto Glacier, which is situated in a predominantly Cambrian carbonate terrain, is 13.4 square kilometres in area. It flows down from the Wapta Icefield at 3,185 metres above sea level over a single icefall at 2,400 metres to its toe at approximately 2,125 metres. On the glacier, daily summer temperatures range from 5° to 16° C in the daytime and from -2° to -4° C at night. Winter temperatures often dip below -30° C.

The valley in which Peyto Lake lies bears the marks of earlier advances of Peyto Glacier. The lake itself is dammed by tree-covered end moraines, which were deposited during a Holocene advance. Lateral moraines and trim lines can also be seen along the valley wall.

From this viewpoint (Figure 118) the most striking feature is Peyto Lake, which derives its colour from the presence of rock flour that is suspended in the water. As meltwater leaves the terminus of the glacier it flows onto the outwash plain in one large channel which continues for approximately two kilometres to the point where it becomes braided and then increasingly branching towards the lake. At the mouth of the braided river a delta is building out into Peyto Lake (Figure 118, centre). Plumes of light grey

Figure 118. Three scenes from the Peyto Lake viewpoint. Left: The Peyto Glacier descends from the Wapta Icefield. Bare lateral moraine and a forested terminal moraine in centre of the photo mark former positions of the ice. Centre: Meltwater transports sediment onto the outwash plain and is gradually filling Peyto Lake. Right: Peyto Lake is dammed by an end moraine deposit.

silt- and clay-laden water extend about 75 metres out into the lake. Scientists have estimated that between 40,000 and 70,000 tonnes of sediment are deposited in Peyto Lake annually. If conditions do not change, the lake could eventually fill up with sediment.

STOP 18: NORTH SASKATCHEWAN RIVER CROSSING

At Saskatchewan Crossing the North Saskatchewan River is joined by the Howse and Mistaya rivers and turns eastward to cross the Front Ranges of the Rockies. In the vicinity of the crossing, the glacial deposits consist mainly of ice stagnation features. About 90 metres southwest (upstream) of the bridge, sections in the north bank of the river show three metres of loess, probably derived from the extensive braided floodplain upstream (Figures 119 and 120).

This locality is well known for the occurrence of Holocene ash layers. Two distinct ash units—Mazama (7,600 years old) and Bridge River (2,435 years old)—occur within these silts (Figure 121). Reworked ash horizons are also present. Identification of the Bridge River and Mazama ashes at this site is based on chemical and mineralogical composition.

At other exposures in the vicinity, St. Helens Y ash (3,600 years old) is also found. The white band of Mazama ash is clearly seen but the Bridge River is diluted by loess, so it is not visible.

Figure 119 (top). Outcrop on the north side of the river at Saskatchewan Crossing, west of the highway. Glacially-derived fluvial gravels form the darker base deposit at the observer's foot. They are overlain by a loess deposit representing deposition of wind-borne fine sediment. Mazama ash forms a light coloured layer between the arrows, and dates the horizon at 7,600 years before present.

Figure 120 (lower left). Detail of the outcrop shown in the left of Figure 119. The fine nature of the loess deposit can be seen clearly, in contrast with the underlying coarse sediment.

Figure 121 (lower right). Detail showing the Mazama ash layer between the arrows. Coin in middle of photo provides scale.

Mazama Ash

loess

fluvial gravel

Mazama Ash

SUNWAPTA PASS AREA

STOP 19: SUNWAPTA PASS AREA AND SASKATCHEWAN GLACIER

Sunwapta Pass

Sunwapta Pass is a one kilometre wide, shallow valley that extends seven kilometres westward from the Banff-Jasper National Park Boundary to the moraines of the Athabasca Glacier. The pass forms the major drainage divide between the Athabasca River draining northward to the Arctic Ocean, and the North Saskatchewan River draining eastward into Hudson Bay. Both rivers have their sources in outlet glaciers of the Columbia Icefield. The Saskatchewan Glacier, feeding the North Saskatchewan River, is the largest outlet glacier from the icefield. It cannot be seen from the highway, but

Figure 122. The Saskatchewan Glacier can be seen from Parker's Ridge.

an excellent view of the glacier with a prominent medial moraine and extensive proglacial outwash plain can be obtained by hiking up Parker's Ridge (Figure 122). The glacier has been actively receding for the last century at a rate of about 50 metres per year.

Hilda Rock Glacier

The Hilda rock glacier (Figure 86, page 71) lies just north of Hilda Creek at the south end of Sunwapta Pass. It emanates from a small cirque at 2,600 metres elevation, descends to 2,150 metres and covers an area of 1.5 square kilometres. The rock glacier is fed by rockfall and snow avalanches from the cliffs above it. Large scale transverse wrinkles or waves on the surface testify to the slow downhill creep of the glacier. Tree ring dating of wood overrun by the snout of the glacier shows that the advance has averaged about 1.6 centimetres per year for at least the last 200, and possibly 400, years. Other studies in the Lake Louise, Moraine Lake and Kananaskis areas have confirmed that rock glaciers show slow forward movement. The reason is probably that the rocks on the surface insulate the ice content of the rock glaciers from summer heat. Insulation is also responsible for the occurrence of rock glaciers at elevations 400 to 600 metres lower than ice glaciers.

Headwater Valleys

The deeply entrenched headwater valleys of the North Saskatchewan drainage are the most spectacular section of the Icefields Parkway. The towering slopes flanking the highway also provide the greatest snow avalanche hazard to the highway. Nearly 70 avalanche tracks run onto or threaten the highway between Tangle Ridge and the North Saskatchewan River Crossing. The most dangerous sites are along the 30-kilometre stretch from the Saskatchewan River Crossing to the Weeping Wall (just south of the hairpin bend in the Banff-Jasper highway) where the road runs along the foot of long open slopes inclined between 25° and 60°, and below the rock slabs on Parker's Ridge at the southern entrance to Sunwapta Pass. Since 1971 avalanche activity along this section has been monitored by Parks Canada, and an avalanche warning and control system was set up.

ATHABASCA GLACIER AND THE COLUMBIA ICEFIELD

STOP 20: ATHABASCA GLACIER

The Athabasca Glacier has been seen and studied by more scientists than any other in Canada. Its accessibility makes it an important stop. Visitors can view the glacier from the Icefields Interpretive Centre, study the education displays, walk to the terminus of the ice, and take a professionally guided tour onto the glacier itself. You should plan to spend some time here.

Setting

The Columbia Icefield covers 325 square kilometres. The ice occupies a plateau surrounded by high mountains, and is about 350 metres thick. The Athabasca Glacier (Figure 123) is just one of six major glaciers draining the Columbia Icefield (Figure 124). It flows from the Icefield's highest elevation, the Snow Dome, located at 3,460 metres elevation, out of sight to the north (right) of the view from the Icefield Centre. In spite of its impressive size, it is not the largest glacier emanating from the icefield.

Figure 123. The Athabasca Glacier descends from the Columbia Icefield over three ice steps. Note the prominent knife-edge lateral moraine on the left resulting from a previous advance.

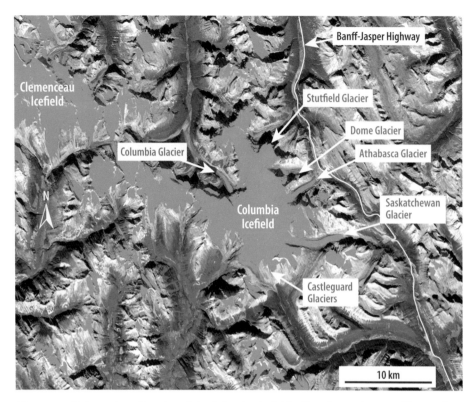

Figure 124. Enhanced satellite view of the Columbia Icefield. Glacial ice is shown in blue, with the six main outlet glaciers labelled. The Columbia Icefield merges with the Clemenceau Icefield to the west.

Figure 125. Athabasca Glacier terminus with warning signs for visitors.

IMPORTANT SAFETY WARNING.

Do not venture onto the ice. No matter how solid the surface looks, there are hidden crevasses beneath the snow cover. Look at the crevasse network shown on Figure 127, and remember that crevasses change location as the glacier moves. If you fall through into a crevasse, your chance of being rescued is extremely small. Visitors have died here. Read the warning signs posted at the terminus (Figure 125). Regardless of what others are doing, do not take a chance.

Structure

The Athabasca Glacier (Figure 127) is about 4.5 kilometres long and descends from the main ice mass over three major rock steps at 2,600, 2,400 and 2,350 metres elevation. Flexure of the ice over each rock step causes a network of transverse crevasses to develop, called an *icefall*. The ice is approximately 300 metres thick as it enters the valley below the lowest ice step. In its lower reaches, the western third of the glacier is debris covered and does not have the appearance of ice.

Ice Flow

Ice flow velocities along the centreline range from about 75 metres per year below the upper icefall to 15 metres per year near the toe. Ice now at the terminus fell as snow on the icefield approximately 200 years ago. The rate can speed up at the height of summer as the ice contact with underlying bedrock is lubricated by meltwater. Tributary glaciers flow eastwards from Mount Andromeda and Mount Athabasca. Friction of the ice along the valley walls causes a system of crevasses to develop, oriented at an angle to the flow direction. During the winter the ice advances slightly, about six to ten metres. However summer melting exceeds this rate, and so the glacier is in retreat.

The terminus is presently at about 2,000 metres elevation (Figure 125). In summer, meltwater pours from the surface, sides and base of the ice (Figure 126). The water enters the Sunwapta River and begins its journey past Jasper through the Athabasca River system on its way to the Arctic Ocean. Several rock outcrops in front of the terminus show striations produced by scraping of rock debris embedded in the ice over the bedrock surface (Figure 128).

Figure 126 (right). The Athabasca Glacier at the height of summer melt. Water courses off the ice surface in meandering streams (top left). It merges with turbulent side streams flowing on the surface of the ice adjacent to a lateral moraine (top right). A large volume of water moves unseen under the ice. It enhances ice movement and emerges at the glacier terminus (bottom). The water is cloudy because it carries fine silt and clay derived from erosion by the debris-laden ice.

Figure 130. Panorama from the Icefields Centre, taken in 2000. The Dome Glacier (right) has receded considerably, because most of its ice supply has been cut off by its high spill point from the icefield. It is now fed mainly by avalanching from the Snow Dome, behind the central peak. Large lateral moraines indicate it merged with the Athabasca Glacier in the past (as recently as 1898).

Past Positions

A century ago, the terminus of the Athabasca Glacier was at the location of the Interpretive Centre and covered the site of the Banff-Jasper highway. Since then, the glacier has been in retreat, and has receded over one kilometre to its position today. Temporary pauses in the retreat are marked by several moraines between the highway and the glacier. Successive positions of the terminus have been mapped (Figure 129).

Figure 129. Aerial photograph of the Athabasca Glacier forefield showing former positions of the glacier terminus as mapped by Brian Luckman (University of Western Ontario) and others. This photo was taken in 1980, before the current Interpretive Centre was constructed.

Dendrochronology plays an important role in dating the ice margin positions. A small section of early eighteenth century moraine occurs at one locality on the west lateral moraine of the Athabasca Glacier where a tree tilted by the glacier in 1714 was discovered (lower left of Figure 129). This advance was probably of similar extent to the 1840s event, as the oldest trees growing on the banks of an abandoned ice-margin channel at the terminus of the Athabasca Glacier date from the middle 1700s.

The forefield of the glacier is still under the influence of cold air descending from the ice and it has not yet been colonized by trees or significant vegetation. Depending on the prevailing weather system, in summer the forefield can be cold and foggy, while a few kilometres along the highway in either direction it is warm and sunny.

The topography of the ice outlet from the Columbia Icefield is an important control on the movement of the terminus. The Dome Glacier occupies the valley immediately north of the Athabasca and is fed by only a narrow passage between the peaks confining the Columbia Icefield. With its access to new ice largely cut off, the Dome Glacier has retreated more than the Athabasca Glacier in the last century, leaving a broad valley with a blanket of ice-cored moraine (Figure 130).

STOP 21: MOUNT KITCHENER VIEWPOINT

This viewpoint offers excellent views of the Sunwapta Valley from the Athabasca Glacier to Stutfield Valley. A large undated landslide of limestone and dolomite from the flanks of Mt. Kitchener (3,498 metres) blocks the Sunwapta Valley at this point (Figure 131). The river has cut a canyon over 50 metres deep through this deposit and the underlying bedrock. In the lower part of this canyon a series of large springs emerges from the landslide debris/bedrock junction forming waterfalls down the canyon wall. Directly across from the viewpoint is the highest point of the Columbia Icefield, the Snow Dome (3,450 metres).

Figure 131. Landslide deposit from Mt. Kitchener. Larger view in Figure 87, page 71.

STOP 22: JONAS CREEK SLIDE

About 1.5 kilometres north of Jonas Creek, a thin veneer of quartzitic landslide debris, 3 to 5 metres thick and originating in a relatively shallow scar on the upper slope of the Endless Chain, extends across the site of the highway. A smaller landslide is also visible on the ridge but it does not reach the highway. A minimum age of 500 to 1,000 years before present is estimated for these two slides, based on growth rates of *Rhizocarpon* sp. lichen found growing on the deposits.

STOP 23: GOAT POINT LAKE DEPOSIT

This stop is at a viewpoint at the top of a 30 metre high bluff of grey glacial lake clays and silts which are often used as a salt-lick by mountain goats. Just south of this stop there is a good exposure of Mazama ash within the lake sediments.

STOP 24: ATHABASCA FALLS

The Athabasca River drops over a quartzite cliff forming a waterfall about 30 metres high (Figure 132). The waterfall has been cutting a gorge since deglaciation of the area at least 12,000 years ago. It is unusual because it is cut through the extremely hard quartzites of the Gog Formation, whereas other major waterfalls in the national parks are on softer and more soluble carbonate rock and shale. The size of the Athabasca River, funneling through this narrow gorge with its entrained load of silt and sand, is responsible for its erosive power.

Figure 132. Athabasca Falls.

STOP 25: MOUNT EDITH CAVELL

Mount Edith Cavell is the type locality of the Little Ice Age Cavell advance. In addition to spectacular scenery, features of interest include modern glaciers and moraines. From the Mount Edith Cavell parking lot a well-maintained loop trail 1.6 kilometres long climbs across a spectacular series of Little Ice Age moraines, then drops down to Cavell Lake and returns along Cavell Creek.

Mount Edith Cavell (3,356 metres) is one of the highest mountains in Jasper National Park. The Cavell Creek valley contains several glaciers which used to form a continuous mass. Angel Glacier spills out of the classic cirque in the east face of Mount Edith Cavell (Figure 133). Although there have been marked changes in the morphology of the hanging tongue, its position changed little from 1962 to 1976. Between 1977 and 1981 the central third of the hanging tongue advanced about 50 metres to the base of the steep cliff. By 1983 this bulge had disappeared and in 1985 the glacier terminated at the 1962-76 position. The small ice mass perched spectacularly on a steep bench on the east face of Cavell seems to have changed little in size since the earliest photographs (1915) and

Figure 133. The Angel Glacier spills from a cirque on Mt. Edith Cavell. Note the lateral moraine from an earlier advance in right foreground.

appears to be in equilibrium. The three remaining glaciers all nestle in the floor of the valley, in the shadow of the east face of Mount Edith Cavell. They exist below the equilibrium line altitude, but persist due to the insulation provided by their heavy coating of rock debris (Figure 134). Cavell Glacier is the largest of these lower glaciers and during the Cavell Advance produced the forefield (Figures 135 and 136) and suite of lateral and terminal moraines near the parking lot.

About 100 to 150 metres south of the trail to the upper viewpoint there are two areas where, on the basis of morphological relationships and lichen cover, small sections of pre-Cavell moraines are preserved outside the Cavell Advance limit. The lichen data for these ridges indicate minimum ages between 733 and 1,660 years. However, based on data from other sites, these deposits are probably much older than these minimum dates.

Figure 134 (top left). Glacial ice in the central Cavell valley, melting into a small lake. Note the deformed annual layers in the ice cliff face and the heavy surface coating of rock debris. With complete melting, the clasts will be deposited onto the forefield plain (Figure 135).

Figure 135 (bottom left). The debris forefield in the Cavell valley. Very little vegetation has taken hold since the debris was let down by melting ice.

Figure 136 (below). Detail of rock debris in the forefield. Small slow-growing lichen patches are beginning to appear. Coin on large centre rock (arrow) provides scale.

Stop 26: Jasper Water Supply Section

This stop is about 100 metres up the Jasper townsite water supply road on the west side of town. Here a portion of the Late Wisconsinan (Marlboro) glacial deposits can be seen. Till deposited at the base of the glacier grades laterally into ice-contact gravels. Older braided stream outwash gravels occur below the till. A radiocarbon date of 29,100 ± 560 years was obtained from wood found in the outwash sands and gravels (Figure 137) and indicates that the overlying till is Late Wisconsinan in age.

Stop 27: Maligne River Valley

The Maligne River drains 880 square kilometres and is one of the major tributaries of the Athabasca River in Jasper National Park. The valley floor and eastern flanks of the valley are developed mainly in limestones and shales. The western flanks consist of sandstones, quartzites and shales. The valley floor, particularly near Maligne Lake, is choked with glacial deposits.

Medicine Lake divides the valley into two distinct but linked hydrological systems. The drainage of the upper valley (70 per

Figure 137. Outcrop on the Jasper water supply road shows outwash gravels capped by lighter coloured till.

cent of the basin) sinks underground in Medicine Lake and re-emerges about 16 kilometres downstream in several springs near and within Maligne Canyon. A separate surface drainage network drains the valley between Maligne Canyon and Medicine Lake. The subsurface drainage is linked to cavities and cave networks produced by solution of carbonate rocks (karst processes) prior to glaciation. The Maligne Valley "hangs" about 90

metres above the main Athabasca Valley. Consequently, the lower Maligne River has cut a deep spectacular gorge (Maligne Canyon) in limestone as it descends to the main valley.

Medicine Lake is intermittent and functions as a simple storage reservoir. During the spring snowmelt period, when the input of the Maligne River exceeds the capacity of the sinks (output), the lake gradually rises to a maximum depth of about 18 metres. At this time the lake overflows around the western end of the landslide at the end of the lake which feeds a surface stream that joins the lower Maligne River. The lake overflows once every two or three years for periods of a few days to over a month in exceptional years. Whether, and how long, this overflow continues depends on the volume and rate of snowmelt in the upper basin. During the latter part of the summer and fall, the lake level gradually drops as output exceeds input. From late fall until the following spring, the lake is empty and the river meanders across the mudflats to sink underground at the northern end of the lake.

STOP 28: ATHABASCA VALLEY SAND DUNES AND LOESS

Beginning 25 kilometres downstream of Jasper townsite, the Athabasca River flows through a series of wide shallow lakes (Jasper and Brûlé lakes). At low water, large areas of fine-grained sediments are exposed to aeolian activity and large, partially stabilized, Holocene, longitudinal sand dunes (20 to 30 metres high) have developed on the eastern shores (Figure 138). Further downstream many sections show a veneer of Holocene loess. Radiocarbon dating indicates one section of loess about 2.5 metres thick has accumulated in the last 2,730 years.

Figure 138. Partially exposed Holocene sand dunes bordering the east side of Brûlé Lake in Jasper National Park.

STOP 29: ROCHE MIETTE SECTION

The stop is located along an unnamed, intermittent creek draining off the north side of Roche Miette. The section is accessible via a pipeline right-of-way that intersects Highway 16 about five kilometres north of the Rocky River bridge. Here is an excellent exposure of an ancient alluvial fan, deposited prior to the Late Wisconsinan ice advance. The fan underlies till, outwash and loess.

Approximately 45 metres of crudely stratified gravel, sand and silt constitute the basal unit of this fan deposit. A non-glacial origin is indicated by the absence of erratics, and current and lithologic data that indicate the sediments were derived from the northwest slopes of Roche Miette.

Overlying the alluvial gravels is a 20-metre unit of moderately to well sorted, and well bedded, outwash gravels (Figure 139) that indicates a source area to the southwest, similar to the present day Athabasca River. The elevation of these gravels (approximately 1,100 metres above sea level) compared to the present day river (about 1,000 metres above sea level) suggests outwash gravels were controlled by a glacier in the Athabasca Valley. About 0.5 to 2 metres of silt interbedded with soils and a Mazama volcanic ash layer overlie the outwash

Figure 139. Alluvial fan deposit at Roche Miette.

Figure 140. Uppermost part of the Roche Miette section showing outwash gravels overlain by a bed of fine greenish-grey loess, the Mazama ash (light band) and several reddish soil horizons.

unit (Figure 140). Intermittent deposition, and possible reworking of volcanic ash occurred during deposition of the loess. Several episodes of soil development and burial occurred.

STOP 30: POCAHONTAS ASH SITE

Rising to the top of the bluff, a short distance south of Highway 16 (less than a kilometre), on the Miette Hot Springs road, is an interesting site that allows the close examination of paleosols, volcanic ash, snails and other fossil material in about 1.5 metres of Holocene loess overlying gravels.

The loess that caps this section consists mainly of well-sorted, massive silts. Terrestrial snail fossils occur throughout. Buried soil horizons are recognized by layers and mottled patches of red and black soil. A prominent white ash bed occurs in the middle of the silts. Dates of about 4,800 years on charcoal 20 centimetres below the ash bed, and about 3,200 years (3,070 radiocarbon years) on charcoal 30 centimetres above the tephra, indicate that the ash probably is the St. Helens Yn (Figure 90, page 74). A 12,900 year old date on shells was obtained from postglacial deposits nearby.

STOP 31: HINTON TERRACES

Glacial outwash gravels at this stop form part of a well developed terrace of the Athabasca River. There are two main terraces in the area (~1,090 metres and ~960 metres elevation) that probably formed during retreat of glaciers up the Athabasca Valley. At Hinton, the terraces are about 30 and 60 metres above river level. The terraces contain pebble to cobble size gravels characterized by a lower trough cross-bedded unit overlain by an upper horizontally bedded unit. The two units may reflect a transition from proximal, rapidly fluctuating flows to more distal, uniform flows as glaciers retreated from the area.

Figure 141. Cross section of a complex drumlin-like feature north of Hinton. Most of the drumlin is composed of till. Black dashed lines indicate planes of internal deformation in the drumlin structure. The darker sediment above the left line is an older bedrock inclusion indicating the erosional nature of this deposit.

STOP 32: HINTON DRUMLINS

Streamlined landforms are widespread in the area northeast of Hinton. The ridges are not regular in form and thus do not meet the same criteria as classical drumlins or flutings. However, they are generally long compared to their width and will be referred to as drumlins. Ridges in close proximity are of markedly different sizes, and some ridges appear to be compound features with a number of superimposed elements. The ridges are subparallel trending down valley, and they presumably parallel the former flow direction of ice close to the valley centre. Ice molded landforms to the east illustrate deflection of the former ice flow, first eastwards and then southwards (Figure 72, page 61). This deflection is attributed to the confluence of Laurentide and Cordilleran ice when the landforms were created.

Forestry road cuts have exposed good sections of the drumlins (Figure 141). Till is the dominant material exposed, but numerous stratified beds reveal that the ridges have a complex internal structure. The till is relatively coarse with a silty matrix. Boulders and pebbles are generally rounded, but locally derived blocks of sandstone are usually angular. Some rocks are striated. The presence of quartzites, carbonates, conglomerates, and sandstones, with some shale and coal clasts, illustrates that the till has a Cordilleran or local origin.

Shear structures and overturned folds are revealed by the clay beds within the drumlin. The clay beds have been sheared and deformed upward from the underlying poorly lithified Tertiary bedrock. Immediately adjacent to these disturbed zones the bedding, as shown by sorted stratified layers, is close to horizontal.

The correspondence between surface form and internal structure of these drumlins rules out an exclusively erosional hypothesis. The internal structures show that folding and shearing played an important role in the up glacier zone. It may be that a pre-existing obstacle or barrier acted as a nucleus for drumlin formation. Thus, the drumlin resulted from subsequent lee side accumulation of debris-rich ice behind this obstacle, and final till deposition occurred by basal melt-out. By this interpretation the relatively horizontal sorted layers were deposited at the same time as the melt-out till. The combination of folding and shearing and lee side deposition then corresponds, in part, to the explanation of drumlin and fluting origin.

STOP 33: EMERSON LAKES ESKER COMPLEX

The Emerson Lake Esker Complex is a series of interconnected ridges arranged approximately north-south with intervening kettle holes and lakes, located on either side of a major logging road northeast of Hinton.

Esker ridges with relief of about 20 metres rise above the adjacent kettle lakes (Figure 142). The eskers are composed of gravel and sand with current indicators pointing to northwest stream flow. The lithology of the gravels, mainly well rounded quartzite, suggests that the eskers originated within the Cordilleran ice. The crests of the eskers rise towards the north and thus have a reversed slope relative to the current. It is, therefore, probable that they formed within the ice either englacially or supraglacially. As differential melting took place, the slope of the gravels and sand became oriented to the north.

Figure 142. A sharp-crested esker of the Emerson Lake esker complex displaying coarse ice-contact gravels along the trail.

SHORT TERM

CLIMATE CHANGE

At the start of this book we discussed some possible causes of long-term climate change, on the scale of millions or tens of millions of years, that bring the globe in and out of glacial periods. However the detailed records of the Quaternary Period (2.6 million years so far) show that there have been continual short-term climate events on a scale of thousands, hundreds or even tens of years. What causes short term fluctuations such as the Younger Dryas cold event? How can a short term warming trend interrupt a long term cooling trend? It is a complex subject with little consensus among climatologists, but we offer a few ideas.

SHORT TERM MECHANISMS

Short-term mechanisms that can cause climate change include: volcanic eruptions (days to years), aerosols and dust clouds from deserts or cultivated farmland (days to years), solar forcing and changes in the amount of irradiance from the Sun (decades to centuries), the El Niño-Southern Oscillation in the Pacific Ocean (a few years at best), changes in the concentration of greenhouse gases in the atmosphere (decades to centuries), and changes in the patterns or modes of ocean circulation (up to approximately a thousand years). The length of the climate variation associated with the mechanism generally increases with the persistence of the event. Several mechanisms may operate simultaneously, leading to very complex climate effects. This list of causes is neither exhaustive nor comprehensive. There are additional mechanisms for historic times, such as land use changes or the human influence on greenhouse gases. There are great gaps in our knowledge and understanding of predictions of future short-term change.

How quickly can changes occur? The Younger Dryas cold period about 13,000 to 11,600 years ago was initiated when a temperature drop of 5-10°C occurred over about a decade. A more recent change in terms of precipitation is the decade known as the Dirty Thirties (~1930-40)

when severe drought occurred in North America. Here we discuss a few of the more common causes of short-term climate change and give examples of how they work, their duration, and where and when these have occurred in the past.

Volcanic Eruptions

Volcanic eruptions that spew dust and gases into the atmosphere cannot be predicted with certainty more than a few days ahead of time. These events can cause global climate change by blocking incoming solar radiation, if the event is large enough to inject tons of dust and gases high into the atmosphere so that the particles can be transported around the Earth by winds (Figure 143). This has happened in the past; however, the effect of these events on temperature change is limited to the length of time the particles remain in the atmosphere (the *residence time*), thus the time span is generally no more than a few years or so and further limited to a small magnitude of temperature change (≤1° C).

Aerosols and Dust Clouds

Aerosols are particulate matter (for example, dust and soot) that enter the atmosphere through dust storms, smoke stacks, fires and wind erosion of cultivated fields. The effect of aerosols on climate is extremely complex, since aerosols can aid in cooling Earth by

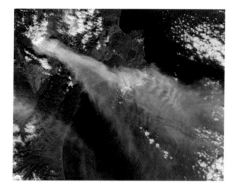

Figure 143. An ash plume streams from a volcano of the Sheveluch complex on eastern Russia's Kamchatka Peninsula in 2004.

reflection of incoming solar radiation, or heat the atmosphere by absorption of radiation and its re-emission directly back into the atmosphere as heat. Aerosols also aid cloud formation by serving as nuclei upon which water vapour will condense. Particle size is larger and concentration higher near the source, so often the effect of aerosols on climate may be regional and short lived rather than global. However, the smaller the particles the longer they stay in the atmosphere and thus influence climate. If aerosol loading is persistent, especially concerning small particles, then the effect on climate will last longer. Ice core studies indicate the time span for such persistence could be on the order of a thousand years. In the Greenland ice cores, elevated levels of particulate matter are correlated with cold climate periods.

Solar Forcing

Variation in solar irradiance can affect climate by changing the amount of energy received by Earth. Sunspots (cooler areas) and faculae (hotter areas) are magnetic disturbances in the plasma near the Sun's surface that increase the emission of visible and ultraviolet radiation by up to 0.2 per cent (Figure 144).

Sunspots wax and wane on a regular cycle of about 11 years. The cycles can be interrupted by periods of minimal magnetic activity and corresponding reduced insolation on Earth. Several quiescent periods occurred from about 1450 to 1800 AD and the decrease in total solar irradiance may have caused or contributed to the Little Ice Age

Additional irradiance cycles occur on approximately 87 and 210-year intervals. These longer changes may interact with Earth-based climate variables to produce complex climate changes.

Recent satellite measurements of total solar irradiance show a slight but significant increase over the previous cycle. If the trend continues, it could cause Earth's average surface temperature to rise by about 0.4° C over the next century.

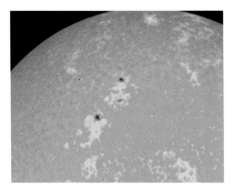

Figure 144. Sunspots (dark) and faculae (white) on the surface of the Sun.

El Niño-La Niña

Perhaps the most well known mechanism of climate change at present is El Niño. The changes from El Niño to La Niña represent alternations in the temperature of the Pacific Ocean that are driven by a change in surface ocean temperature and tropical wind directions. In a normal situation, tropical winds blowing from east to west push warm surface waters toward the western Pacific Ocean. Cold ocean water from the depths of the ocean then rises to the surface on the west coast of South America. As a result, the water in the western Pacific Ocean at 29°C is about six degrees warmer than water in the eastern Pacific Ocean, and even sea level is slightly higher in the west than the east by about 0.5 metres. This area of warm water is known as the Western Pacific Warm Pool and is a major influence on global climate. The degree to which the warm pool extends along the equator to the east determines if an El Niño or a La Niña will occur. El Niño occurs when Warm Pool water flows much further to the east than normal, while La Niña describes warm water extending less far across the tropical Pacific than normal. This change in ocean temperature causes variations in atmospheric temperature and precipitation in many areas of the world. The ability of meteorologists to anticipate and predict the magnitude of change and the length of time over which the change will occur is constantly improving.

Greenhouse Gases

The variation in greenhouse gas concentrations in the atmosphere and their relationships to natural and human causes is at the forefront of international discussion. Although there is not complete consensus on the role of human actions in increasing the concentration relative to natural variation, the effect of elevated (or reduced) levels of greenhouse gases on climate is indisputable. The two most abundant greenhouse gases, water vapour and carbon dioxide, contribute about 65 per cent and 25 per cent, respectively, of the present natural greenhouse effect, while methane, nitrous oxide and other trace gases contribute the remainder.

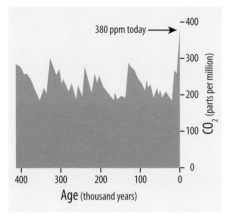

Figure 145. Change in atmospheric carbon dioxide concentration over the last 400,000 years. The data are from the Antarctic Vostok ice core, and cover four glacial-interglacial cycles. CO_2 varied between 180 and 280 parts per million by volume (ppmv) for most of the time, before rising to 380 ppmv over the last century.

The change of CO_2 concentration in step with climate, from higher levels in interglacial times to lower values in glacial times, is remarkable (Figure 145). However, correlation does not prove causation. Atmospheric CO_2 concentration is a product of many different physical and chemical processes that affect carbon cycling between the land, oceans and atmosphere.

The changes in concentration of CO_2 and other greenhouse gases in the atmosphere during the last 50 years are dramatic and suggest that human-caused emissions will contribute to climate change. At issue, however, is the amount of change that is natural versus the amount caused by human actions. The debate is ongoing.

Ocean Circulation

As mentioned in the opening chapter of this book, thermohaline ocean circulation has a strong influence on climate (see Figure 2, page 2). Climate change can cause dramatic modifications to ocean thermohaline circulation, which further exacerbate climate. For example, as the climate warms and glaciers melt, more fresh water flows to the North Atlantic Ocean, forming a cap of less dense fresh water on the ocean surface. The warm, salty Gulf Stream mixes with this fresh water cap, making it less dense than it is normally. Hence, the northern arm of ocean circulation that usually descends to the deep ocean either ceases to descend or descends to shallower depths. Areas once warmed by the Gulf current will cool. For example, Ireland is at about the same latitude as southern Alaska, yet currently has a much warmer climate. If the North Atlantic heat conveyor is inhibited, then the climate of Ireland and the rest of the countries in northern Europe could cool dramatically. Thus our present warming can induce a regional cold spell, which some climate models suggest could spread worldwide.

The rapidity of this change in ocean circulation may be the cause for the Younger Dryas cold period (see Figure 80, page 67), which occurred as massive amounts of cold fresh water were released from the North American continent into the North Atlantic as the Laurentide Ice Sheet melted. There is abundant climate proxy evidence that the Younger Dryas cooling propagated to other areas of the globe, including western Canada and the Rocky Mountains, so ocean circulation changes in the North Atlantic could be felt in areas far away.

There are many questions yet to ask and problems to solve regarding short-term climate change.

FUTURE

CLIMATE CHANGE

Scientists cannot predict future climate change with a high degree of certainty, but that is exactly what they are asked to do by politicians and economists, because thousands of lives and billions of dollars are at stake. Future negative effects of a warming climate include rising sea levels, depleted agriculture, reduced water flows, increased health hazards, turbulent weather and social strains. Not all areas will suffer negative effects. For example, some regions will receive increased rainfall which could enhance agriculture. Understanding climate change and differentiating the natural causes of climate change from human contribution is one of the most pressing social and economic issues.

General Circulation Models

The tool of choice for predicting future climate is a climate model. Most popular are computer software programs called General Circulation Models (GCM). GCMs divide the globe into a grid upon which layers of cells are applied vertically to define the characteristics of the ocean and atmosphere (Figure 146). A model using a grid of 4 degrees by 5 degrees and 23 layers has about 150,000 cells. The GCM must assume or calculate values for temperature, pressure, clouds, insolation, atmospheric and oceanic chemistry and a host of other parameters for each cell and the effect of each cell upon its neighbouring cells. The computation load of a GCM is huge, so many simplifying assumptions are applied. The models must be tested for reasonableness by comparing model calculations to climate data collected during the present or recent past.

The GCMs are started in the past and checked against known temperature and precipitation trends indicated by the proxy data. This helps to calibrate the software before it is used to predict future change. The results of a climate model prediction are not factual; the predictions are only suggestions of what may occur given the limitations and assumptions in the model. Climate models are not able yet to mimic all the changes that occur in nature. The models are run over

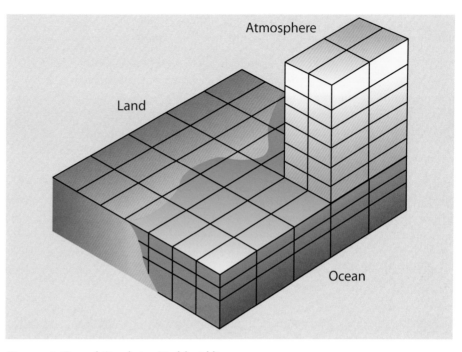

Figure 146. General Circulation Model gridding.

and over with slight variation of input parameters each time to provide a range of possible outcomes. The most complex models—those which are potentially the most realistic—require the use of supercomputers, and can only be run a limited number of times due to the cost of computer time. It can take a full day of computation to forecast two or three years of future climate.

The most notable measure of long term past and future climate comes from the Milankovitch theory of climate

change (see pages 5 to 7). Changes in the orbital parameters have been calculated for the past few million years and into the future. Orbital calculations indicate that insolation is expected to vary one to two per cent over the next 25,000 years. We should not expect such small variation acting alone to cause much change in climate. However, this variation in insolation can lead to larger changes if greenhouse gas concentrations increase. One unknown in models of future climate is the atmospheric concentration of greenhouse gases and how to factor in human perturbations of gas concentration. The Milankovitch theory predicts that we are in a long-term warming trend continuing for the next 50,000 years, to be followed by a return to cool conditions (dependant upon the greenhouse gas concentration). The theory cannot predict short-term changes in climate that may occur over a few decades or centuries.

Variability in earth-atmosphere systems complicates the prediction of short-term climate trends. Short-term cycles superimposed on longer term cycles create complexity in the climate system and add to the difficulty of building comprehensive model simulations.

What do some of the climate models predict for short-term climate change? The United Nations Intergovernmental Panel on Climate Change (IPCC) 2001 report, which considered Earth as a whole, predicted the following changes.

- An average global temperature rise ranging from 1.4 to 5.8°C over the period from 1990 to 2100.

- The increase in mean temperature will lead to more frequent extreme high temperatures and less frequent extreme low temperatures.

- Night-time low temperatures in many regions will increase more than daytime highs, thus reducing the diurnal temperature range.

- Daily variability of temperature in winter will decrease, and variability in summer temperature in Northern Hemisphere mid-latitude areas will increase.

- There will be a general decrease in summer soil moisture in mid-continent areas due to a combination of increased temperature and evaporation exceeding precipitation.

- The intensity of individual precipitation events will increase.

FUTURE CLIMATE CHANGE IN THE ALPINE ENVIRONMENT

Local differences from the IPCC predictions should be expected. Anyone who has spent time in the Rockies knows that mountain weather is characterized by high variability, both in time and space. There can be hot summer days and there can be snow in August. Visitors travelling the Icefields Parkway can leave Jasper in pleasant conditions only to experience sleet and fog at the Columbia Icefield and sun again at Lake Louise. Mountain climate—weather averaged over decades

or centuries—is similarly variable, with evidence for both colder and warmer periods prevailing at different times within the current interglacial period.

General circulation models are concerned with global change; they do not predict climate change for specific areas such as the Rockies. In a GCM where Earth's surface is divided into a grid of 4,000 rectangles, the Canadian Rockies would fit inside a single one. Worse yet, since the Rockies trend northwest-southeast, they do not fit neatly within one cell of a regular grid and they would be averaged with adjacent topographic regions in a regularly-gridded GCM. Nevertheless, with the global warming implied by GCMs, it is possible to predict likely changes to the alpine environment.

In mountains with mild winter temperatures, such as the southern Rockies, climate warming will bring higher winter temperatures. With the temperature increase may come higher precipitation. This will result in increased snowfall at high elevations, a rise in the winter snowline, and precipitation as rain at lower elevations. Mountains with cold winter temperatures will see increased snowfall as well. Overall, the mountains will see a redistribution of the timberline and the snowpack.

Timberline

The alpine and sub-alpine zones occur above the timberline. Timberline is not a discrete break; rather, it is a transition zone from the substantial forest cover of lower elevations to the absence of trees higher up. Timberline is controlled by summer temperatures and the duration of the winter snowpack. It is sensitive to local conditions such as wind, moisture and sun exposure. Tree growth requires light snowfall or early melt together with at least two months of warm summer temperatures. In the Canadian Rockies, timberline elevation varies from about 2,100 metres in the south to 1,500 metres at the Yukon border.

In a warming climate, the timberline will rise to higher elevations. The alpine zone will disappear from lower elevation mountains and its area will be reduced on those of higher elevation, just as it did in the Holocene hypsithermal (Figure 83, page 69). The rise in timberline will be a slow process due to the lag time between the disappearance of snow and the development of the soils necessary to support trees.

Avalanches are usually initiated on slopes above timberline. In the long term, a rise in the timberline will provide stability to the snowpack and reduce the frequency of avalanches. This is important to human activity. The Trans-Canada Highway in the Rogers Pass area of Glacier National Park crosses more than 140 avalanche paths.

Snowpack Changes

Regardless of whether or not precipitation increases, the overall volume of water stored in the snowpack may be less than that of today because of the reduced total area of the snowpack caused by the rise in timberline. Areas at lower elevations, including some ski resorts, will experience warmer temperatures and more rain in winter.

Snowpack—not glacial melt—is the prime natural fresh water reservoir supplying the foothills and prairies through the year. As a storage mechanism, snowpack provides water to the prairies in spring and summer, when demand from agriculture and other human activities is at its peak. With climate warming, more runoff will occur in winter, lessening the water supply later in the year when it is needed most. Warmer temperatures combined with low summer and autumn flows could increase the frequency and severity of drought on the prairies. Rather than exerting a positive influence through a longer growing season, warming could have a negative effect on prairie agriculture.

Drainage from the western slopes of the Rockies into the Columbia River will be reduced, affecting summer and autumn hydroelectric generation capacity or the spring salmon breeding run, depending upon how the water releases from dams along the river are managed.

The snowpack changes are significant globally. Approximately one sixth of the world's population, accounting for one quarter of the global gross domestic product, lives in areas dominated by a snowmelt hydrologic cycle.

Nivation hollows are formed by alpine snow patches that persist well into summer. A combination of processes involving freeze-thaw cycles, meltwater and soil creep produces broad depressions that are sparsely vegetated due to their short exposure time prior to the onset of winter. Alpine ice patches survive year-round in nivation hollows and gentle north-facing slopes, and warmer temperatures will reduce their size. As snow patches melt, they may reveal paleoenvironmental information.

In southern Yukon, melting ice patches exhibit annual layers rich in caribou dung, some in areas where caribou have not been seen for almost 70 years. Radiocarbon dates show the ice patches served as gathering places for caribou

Figure 147. Hunting implement (hafted foreshaft), 5,200 years old, was recovered from a melting alpine ice patch. Length is 29 cm.

Figure 148. Small hourglass-shaped slump caused by melting of ground ice in wet soil.

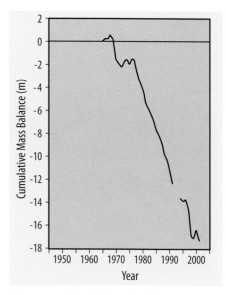

Figure 149. Mass balance for the Peyto Glacier shows a net loss of 18 metres of water equivalent in 35 years.

seeking relief from the biting insects of summer over the last 9,000 years. A gap in the dates from 7,600 to 5,600 years before present suggests that the ice patches were severely reduced in area during the Holocene hypsithermal, and not useful as refuges.

Archaeological work in southern Yukon has also recovered hunting implements made of antler, bone, wood and stone from several melting ice patches (Figure 147). The implements indicate that humans used the caribou for food throughout the postglacial period. The absence of caribou in recent years demonstrates the effect that future climate warming will have on the distribution of prey species and the humans that depend upon them for subsistence.

Frozen Ground

Perennially frozen ground, or permafrost, occurs in parts of the northern Rockies and helps to stabilize moisture-laden soils on low slopes. Warmer temperatures will bring a reduction in permafrost and ground ice lenses, leading to small-scale slumps (Figure 148).

Permanent Snow and Ice

Whether a glacier advances or retreats depends upon its mass balance—the net difference between water added as snow during winter and water lost during the summer melt. A glacier is never in balance. Rather, each year shows a positive or negative balance. Graphing the annual mass balances through time gives a picture of whether a glacier is growing or shrinking (Figure 149).

Glacial advance after an increase in mass is usually delayed a few years, since it takes time for the pressure

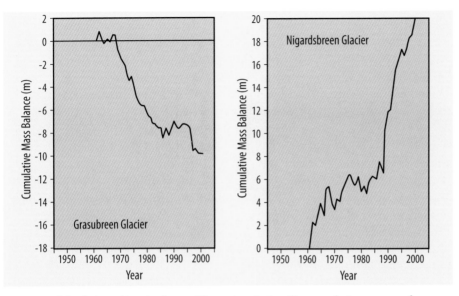

Figure 150. Mass balance histories for two Norwegian glaciers illustrate the importance of microclimate on glacier growth or retreat. The Grasubreen Glacier shows a negative balance while that of the Nigardsbreen is positive.

Figure 151. Barren glacial forefields left by receding glaciers like the Athabasca Glacier (above) will affect the scenic value of the landscape, for better or for worse, depending on the viewer's opinion.

effect of increased snow loading in the accumulation area to be transmitted to the toe of the glacier by ice flow. In contrast, the effect of a negative mass balance year is usually immediately evident in increased melt at the terminus.

Glaciers worldwide have generally retreated over the last century. In a warming climate, glacial mass balance will be determined by the interaction of increased snowfall in the accumulation area and increased melt below the equilibrium line. Individual glaciers are affected by their local or microclimate (Figure 150), so overall predictions are difficult to make. However glaciers at lower elevations, where the equilibrium line is already near the mountain summit, are likely to disappear. Retreat on higher elevation glaciers will replace impressive ice fronts with barren rocky forefields, affecting the aesthetic value of the scenery, perhaps with implications for tourism (Figure 151).

There are geohazards associated with increased melting. In the forefields and lower portions of the ice there will be an increase in lakes impounded by ice dams or ice-cored moraine. Ice can fail by melting, fracturing or even floating off its bed due to the pressure of meltwater lakes. The till comprising moraines is loose, porous material that can be eroded easily by waves or overtopped by enhanced melt. Both these situations can lead to sudden failure and flash floods of water and debris, especially in late summer. This type of flood is more destructive than those due to seasonal rainfall, but they are also short-lived and less frequent.

CONCLUSION

As we enter the twenty-first century, climate change is becoming an important factor in public awareness. Political initiatives to combat the social and economic effects of changing climate will affect the lives of everyone. Media reports often portray climate change in terms of extremes, with little or no space devoted to explaining the spectrum of future climate scenarios or the range of uncertainty accompanying predictions.

In this book we have focused on climate change in the Canadian Rocky Mountains over a recent, geologically short, period of Earth history. Although evidence of climate change is spectacularly exposed in the mountain scenery, it is not straightforward to interpret. Most of the interpretation relies on the use of proxy data, for which we have covered the most important sources and dating methods. Evidence gathered in mountain fieldwork is integrated with global sediment and ice data, and even astrophysical considerations, allowing us to arrive at a reconstructed glacial history of the Rockies over the last 30,000 years.

We hope this book has given you a better understanding of the scientific method, its triumphs and its limitations. We encourage you to visit the Rockies with a new perspective on the scenery.

Road Log Stop Coordinates

The coordinates for Road Log stops are provided for use with maps and global positioning systems.

Stop Number	Location	Latitude	Longitude
1	Morley Flats Drumlins	51° 06' 40.30" N	114° 59' 49.14" W
2	Morley Flats Esker	51° 04' 58.32" N	115° 03' 38.08" W
3	Morley Flats Kame	51° 05' 09.51" N	115° 03' 51.11" W
4	Lac des Arcs, Sand Bluffs	51° 03' 05.72" N	115° 09' 57.69" W
5	Outwash	51° 03' 51.77" N	115° 17' 19.82" W
6	Carrot Creek	51° 09' 03.04" N	115° 25' 38.53" W
7	Powerhouse	51° 11' 42.75" N	115° 29' 24.48" W
8	Tunnel Mountain Hoodoos	51° 11' 16.69" N	115° 31' 14.86" W
9	Bow Falls	51° 09' 59.32" N	115° 33' 36.35" W
10	Highway 1A Slump	51° 14' 12.57" N	115° 49' 20.07" W
11	Castle Mountain Lookout	51° 14' 26.90" N	115° 51' 26.93" W
12	Moraine Lake	51° 19' 39.74" N	116° 10' 48.61" W
13	Moraine Lake Road	51° 20' 57.99" N	116° 10' 17.54" W
14	Lake Louise	51° 25' 03.67" N	116° 13' 02.00" W
15	Kicking Horse River	51° 24' 09.50" N	116° 29' 04.48" W
16	Crowfoot Glacier	51° 39' 47.58" N	116° 26' 18.52" W
17	Peyto Glacier and Peyto Lake	51° 42' 59.67" N	116° 30' 23.31" W
18	North Saskatchewan River Crossing	51° 58' 12.07" N	116° 43' 18.91" W
19	Sunwapta Pass and Saskatchewan Glacier	52° 12' 09.85" N	117° 08' 20.09" W
20	Athabasca Glacier and Columbia Icefield	52° 13' 13.49" N	117° 13' 51.03" W
21	Mount Kitchener	52° 16' 48.31" N	117° 18' 46.83" W
22	Jonas Creek	52° 25' 56.82" N	117° 24' 33.67" W
23	Goat Point	52° 36' 47.29" N	117° 50' 28.71" W
24	Athabasca Falls	52° 39' 53.30" N	117° 53' 05.63" W
25	Mount Edith Cavell	52° 41' 14.11" N	118° 03' 21.48" W
26	Jasper Water Supply	52° 52' 18.29" N	118° 06' 16.86" W
27	Maligne River Valley	52° 48' 02.50" N	117° 41' 23.18" W
28	Athabasca Valley Dunes and Loess	53° 04' 31.06" N	118° 03' 06.84" W
29	Roche Miette	53° 11' 00.47" N	117° 57' 18.76" W
30	Pocahontas Ash	53° 12' 03.43" N	117° 55' 22.09" W
31	Hinton Terraces	53° 26' 29.46" N	117° 32' 36.37" W
32	Hinton Drumlins	53° 33' 18.44" N	117° 20' 38.79" W
33	Emerson Lakes Esker Complex	53° 44' 12.23" N	117° 07' 02.78" W

Glossary of Terrain Terminology

A

Ablation – Where applied to glaciers, a loss of ice by melting, evaporation, sublimation or calving of icebergs.

Ablation till – Till deposited from a stagnating glacier by the process of ablation.

Alluvial fan – A gently sloping accumulation of poorly sorted coarse sand and gravel deposited by a stream descending from a high valley onto a lowland, at which point the material accumulates in a fan or cone shape.

Alluvium – Any unconsolidated poorly to well sorted stratified detrital material consisting of gravel, sand, silt or clay deposited by a stream in a fan shape at the base of an upland or as part of the stream bed, or floodplain.

Arête – A narrow rocky, knife-edged ridge formed by two adjoining cirque glaciers where glaciers erode the wall between the cirques.

B

Basal till – Till deposited at the base of a moving or stagnant glacier characterized by pebbles or cobbles with their long axis parallel to the direction of glacial flow.

Bed – A unit of layered rock, primarily sedimentary, separated from the material above and below by boundary planes.

Bedrock – A generally consolidated deposit either exposed at the surface or underlying surficial, unconsolidated deposits of sediment or soil.

Bluff – A high bank, cliff or bold headland with a broad precipitous face overlooking a land surface or a body of water.

Boulder – A subrounded to rounded rock fragment with a diameter larger than about 256 mm diameter with no upper size limit.

Braided stream – A stream that flows in a channel, subdivided into several narrow channels which successively meet and subdivide, resembling the strands of a braid.

Break-in-slope – A change in the angle of slope along a valley wall, indicating differential erosion, commonly marking the upper limit of a former valley glacier. Breaks-in-slope commonly form longitudinal lines separating a lower slope angle above from a steeper slope angle below.

C

Carbonate rock – A group of rocks composed primarily of carbonate (CO_3). If the rock contains a high proportion of Ca, it is called limestone ($CaCO_3$). If enough magnesium is present it is called dolomite ($CaMgCO_3$).

Chert – Generally a hard, extremely dense microcrystalline sedimentary rock consisting mainly of quartz crystals less than about 30 microns (0.03 mm) in diameter.

Cirque – A rounded basin, shaped like an amphitheatre or a half-bowl cut into the side of the mountain, with steep walls and a flat or gently sloping floor, formed by cirque glaciers.

Clay – The term is used in two senses: 1) to describe a group of largely platy minerals typical in soils and often formed by the chemical transformation from other common minerals, and 2) used to describe particles of sediment that are smaller than 0.002 mm, which cannot be seen by the naked eye.

Cobble – A subrounded to rounded rock fragment between 64 mm and 256 mm diameter.

Col – A relatively smooth divide between two cirques.

Colluvium – Soil or loose fragmented rock deposited primarily by mass movement and found at the base of a steep slope or cliff. Colluvium differs from alluvium in that alluvial deposition is associated with water, whereas colluvium is associated with movement primarily by gravity.

Conglomerate – A coarse-grained clastic sedimentary rock consisting of rounded to subrounded granule pebbles, cobbles and boulders set in a fine-grained matrix of sand or silt (the consolidated equivalent of gravel).

Cordilleran –In Canada, it represents a structural geological province consisting of the mountainous terrain from the Rocky Mountains in the east to the Coast Mountains in the west.

Crevasse – A large V-shaped crack, break, crevice or fissure where tensile forces ('pull apart forces') in a glacier have exceeded the strength of the ice.

Crevasse filling – Sediment or glacial debris that fills a V-shaped crevasse in a glacier that may invert to a roughly teepee-shaped ridge, after the glacier melts.

Cross-bedding – Refers to beds that are inclined at an angle to the main planes of stratification (same as cross-stratification).

D

Detritus (also **detrital**) – Loose rock and mineral fragments such as boulders, cobbles, pebbles, sand, silt and clay derived directly from older rocks by mechanical means such as disintegration or abrasion, and moved from their places of origin.

Dip – The angle that a surface such as a bedding plane or fault plane makes with an imaginary horizontal line; dip is measured perpendicular to strike and is generally the direction that free water would flow on a sloping surface.

Dip slope – The gently sloping surface coincident with the bedding plane surface of the rock composing an escarpment.

Dolomite – A rock type consisting of calcium magnesium carbonate ([CaMg]CO$_3$)

Drift (also **glacial drift**) – When applied to glaciers, refers to all materials deposited directly by glaciers or by glacial meltwater in streams or lakes.

Drumlin – A glacially formed hill, from a few to 50 metres in height (most commonly between 15 to 25 metres) having an oval outline in plain view and consisting of glacial deposits (for example, till or gravel) in a streamlined form. The long axis is parallel to the direction of ice movement with most drumlins having a blunt nose at their up-stream (stoss) side, that tapers downstream (lee). They are commonly a few hundred metres to over a kilometre in length and up to tens of metres wide. Streamlined bedrock that takes the shape of a drumlin is called a rock drumlin.

Dune – A ridge, hummock or mound of loose, granular material, commonly sand, transported, deposited and modified by wind.

E

Eolian (also **aeolian**) – A landform formed or deposited by the action of wind.

End moraine – A moraine that accumulates at the end or terminus of a glacier, which makes a ridge-like form, composed of glacial material. An end moraine may build along any part of the margin of an active glacier. Most end moraines are elongate, commonly arcuate ridges or groups of subparallel ridges from 3 to 70 metres high, oriented transverse to glacier flow. Many arcuate ridges have an irregular surface and are in places discontinuous.

Englacial –Rock fragments embedded or carried within the glacier. Englacial till, although commonly difficult to identify, is derived from this material.

Erosional surface – Any surface that is not an original depositional surface and has been modified by erosional processes.

Esker – An elongated, generally sinuous, continuous or discontinuous ridge or series of discontinuous mounds composed of stratified sand and gravel with or without a cover of till. Eskers are formed from subglacial (below a glacier), englacial (within the glacier) or supraglacial (on top of a glacier) streams flowing in an ice tunnel or in a channel on top of the ice when the glacier is stagnant or nearly stagnant.

F

Fault – A fracture or zone of fractures in rock or coherent surficial material along which discernable displacement of the opposite sides of the fracture has occurred. A fracture is a crack in a rock where there is no displacement.

Firn – The transition between snow and ice, and older than one summer's melt. Firn is formed as more snow is added on top of the previous year's winter precipitation, resulting in the deeper layers of snow taking on a compact, granular texture. As more snow accumulates, firn will change into ice.

Floodplain – The strip of relatively smooth, flat lying land immediately bordering a stream or river which during a flood is covered by water. Floodplains are usually composed of clay and silt, but may contain gravel and sand.

Fluting – A general term referring to narrow, shallow furrow-like features that are long in profile and usually come in multiple sets of parallel furrows. Flutes formed by glacial flow are shallow, narrow and long but can be meters deep and wide, and hundreds of meters in length (e.g., giant flutes). Flutes are created parallel to glacial flow. The ridges separating the furrows resemble elongated drumlins. Flutes are generally formed in till but may be in bedrock or other glacial material.

Fluvial –Pertaining to a river or stream.

Fold – A pronounced bend, flexure, or wave in a rock plane such as a bedding plane.

Foothills – A region of relatively low hills at the base of, or fringing, a mountain range.

Forefield – The area in front of the terminus of a glacier.

G

Glacial erratic – Any rock fragment lithologically different from the bedrock surface on which it lies either free or embedded in surficial material, and which has been transported from its place of origin by glacial ice or an iceberg. The term excludes rock fragments in stream deposits.

Glacier – Body of ice formed by recrystallization of snow and by refreezing of meltwater and firn lying wholly or mostly on land and showing evidence of present or former flow.

Glacial valley – Found in mountainous areas where the valley between mountain ranges has been glacially eroded, producing a valley profile roughly shaped like the letter 'U' from the original 'V' shape.

Glacial trough – See U-shaped valley.

Glaciofluvial – Pertaining to glacier meltwater streams or to the deposits and landforms produced by glaciofluvial streams.

Granules – Particles that are between 2 mm and 4 mm in diameter.

Gravel – Strictly speaking, gravel refers to a size classification of sedimentary particles that may include granules (2–4 mm diameter), pebbles (4–64 mm), cobbles (64–256 mm) and to a lesser extent boulders (>256 mm). Lithification of the particles will generally form a conglomerate. The term is often loosely applied to any unconsolidated sediment consisting predominately of pebbles with or without particles of other grade sizes.

Ground moraine – Glacial material that accumulated beneath an active or stagnant glacier, having low relief (generally less than 2 metres).

H

Hanging valley – A glacial valley whose mouth is at a higher elevation than the floor of the main valley into which it leads.

Hoodoo – A tall column or columns of resistant sedimentary rock, often with a cap of harder rock that protects the underlying softer rock from erosion. Hoodoos are found on or near cliffs and are eroded by wind and water. In the Canadian Rockies, they are commonly composed of relatively resistant till that overlies glacial outwash gravels.

Horn – Found in mountainous areas and refers to a sharp-pointed, pyramidal-shaped rock at the summit of a mountain formed by the erosion of three or more adjoining glaciers, often cirque glaciers. Each of the faces of the horn is coincident with the head wall of a cirque. The name is derived from the famous Matterhorn peak in the Swiss Alps.

Hummock – Any small, rounded rise of more or less equidimensional or conical shape, but not constituting a ridge (also knoll, mound or hillock).

Hummocky moraine – Moraine formed from stagnant glacial ice consisting of an apparently random assemblage of knobs, kettles, hummocks, ridges and depressions without pronounced parallelism or orientation of these elements.

I

Ice-contact sediments – Refers to stream deposits that are laid down in contact with stagnant or near stagnant ice. Kames, eskers and crevasse fillings are examples of ice-contact sediments.

Ice-cored – Usually refers to a stagnant moraine that still contains ice.

Icefall – Highly crevassed ice that is flowing over a steep slope or rock step.

Ice-marginal channel (meltwater channel) – Refers to a stream channel cut by glacial meltwater, commonly into bedrock, and abutting the margin of a glacier either in front of the glacier or on its side.

Ice sheet – A generally domed-shaped mass of continuous ice and snow over an area in excess of 50,000 km^2. The ice sheet will spread outward in all directions from its main accumulation area and is not confined by the underlying topography. Presently, the most famous ice sheets are in Greenland and Antarctica.

Ice stream – A current of ice that flows more or less rapidly than adjacent ice. Also used as a general term for a valley glacier.

Igneous rock – Rock formed by the solidification (crystallization) from lava at the Earth's surface or sea floor, or magma below the surface.

K

Kame – A short, irregular ridge, hill or mound composed chiefly of stratified sand and gravel deposited by meltwater in contact with a glacier at its front or side, or within or upon a glacier, and subjected to modification of its form through subsequent slumping by melting of ice in contact with the kame. A kame complex is a group of closely associated kames.

Karst – Refers to a type of surface topography produced in regions of extensive limestone, dolomite, marble or gypsum by the dissolving action of groundwater on the rocks. The dissolving action may form sinkholes at the surface, and caves and tunnels in the subsurface.

Kettle – A basin or bowl-shaped closed depression or hollow in glacial drift which resulted from the melting of a buried or partially buried mass, lump or lens of ice that became detached from the main body of the glacier.

L

Lacustrine – Pertaining to a lake or its characteristics such as fauna, flora, landforms or deposits.

Laminated – Used here as the thinnest recognizable layer of original deposition in a sediment, commonly 0.05-1.00 mm in thickness.

Landslide – A comprehensive term used to designate a process of sediment movement and resultant landforms associated with down slope or lateral mass movement of natural masses of soil, rock or loose sediment due to gravity. Movement of the mass may be dry or associated with water. Included in the broad usage of the term are avalanche, debris slide, earth flow, mass wasting, mudflow, mudslide, rock fall, rock slide, slump, talus and topple. Landslides may also occur under water.

Lateral moraine – A moraine ridge along the flank of a glacial lobe, particularly one occupying a valley, composed of debris glacially eroded off the valley wall and rockfall from mountain slopes onto the ice.

Lee – Used here to indicate the slope of a hill or knob that faces away from an advancing glacier, i.e., the downstream side of a glacier.

Lens – A deposit bounded by converging surfaces, thick in the middle and thinning out toward the edges, resembling a convex lens.

Limestone – A rock formed of calcium carbonate ($CaCO_3$).

Lithification – The process by which loose sediments are converted into sedimentary rock: lithification includes compaction, consolidation and cementation.

Lithology – The physical character of a rock or unconsolidated rock material such as color, grain size or mineralogical composition.

Loess – A homogeneous, visibly non-stratified, well sorted yellowish- to buff-colored eolian (i.e., windblown) deposit consisting primarily of silt-sized particles with subordinate amounts of fine sand and clay sized particles. The most extensive deposits of loess on Earth are found in the Loess Plateau of north-central China.

Longitudinal sand dune – A sand dune that forms an elongated ridge parallel to the dominant wind direction.

M

Marginal crevasse – A crevasse that develops near the glacier margin, oriented roughly perpendicular to the direction of ice flow.

Mass wasting – A general term for the slow movement down slope of rock or soil due to gravity (see also landslide).

Medial moraine – A moraine ridge within a valley glacier, parallel to its sides and formed by the union of lateral moraines of two coalescing glaciers.

Metamorphic rock – Rocks formed in the Earth's crust below the surface by the transformation of existing rocks and minerals into rocks and minerals of different composition and/or texture as a result of high temperature or pressure or both.

Moraine – A variably thick, glacial landform composed commonly of till that usually covers underlying bedrock or other material. It may be relatively flat at its surface or exhibit a variety of surficial shapes such as hummocks, mounds or ridges. The term is also used with a modifier, as in the case of ground moraine, end moraine, lateral moraine, recessional moraine and terminal moraine.

Mudstone – A general term used to describe a very fine-grained, massive sedimentary rock composed largely of clay minerals or clay-sized particles.

N

Nivation – All processes of erosion associated with an immobile and patchy snow cover of variable size, generally in a periglacial environment (i.e., near a glacier) or areas of perennial snow cover.

Nivation hollow – A small depression or hollow occupied during part of the year by a small snow bank or snow patch and in which the processes of nivation are operative, which includes freeze-thaw, penetration by meltwater, and frost wedging. The nivation hollow may be a precursor to a cirque.

Nunatak – A highland partially submerged by an ice sheet or an isolated hill or peak rising above the surface of a glacier.

O

Outcrop – Part of a geological formation that appears at the surface of the Earth.

Outwash – Mostly flat-lying gravelly and sandy stratified drift washed out from a glacier by its meltwater and deposited at and beyond the margin of a glacier.

P

Paleosol (also **palaeosol**) – In general terms a paleosol is an old soil either buried beneath the modern soil or exhumed to the surface (derived from Latin, *paleo* meaning old; *sol* meaning earth).

Pebble – A size classification of a sedimentary rock fragment, often with subrounded to rounded edges that are larger than a granule (2–4 mm diameter) and smaller than a cobble (64–256 mm diameter).

Periglacial – Landforms or processes near a glacier but not in contact with the glacier.

Plain – A comparatively flat or slightly undulating surface of land, generally at a low elevation. High elevation plains are usually termed plateaus.

Plateaus – An extensive and elevated tract of comparatively flat or level land.

Proglacial – An area in front of a glacier or ice sheet.

Q

Quartzite – A hard sandstone consisting mainly of quartz grains that have been solidly cemented.

R

Recessional moraine – An end moraine built during a temporary but significant halt or minor re-advance of an ice front during a period of overall glacial recession or retreat.

Reticulated network – Used here to indicate a latticed network of glaciers.

Roche mountonnée – A rock outcrop with a whaleback form, the long axis of which is orientated in the direction of ice movement, and which was streamlined by glacial abrasion to produce a gently inclined, smoothed and polished, striated stoss (upstream) end and a steep, abruptly broken, rough and shattered lee (downstream) side.

Rock flour – Very fine powder (usually clay sized particles) formed when rocks embedded in a glacier abrade the underlying bedrock or rock. When suspended in glacial lakes, it gives the water its characteristic turquoise appearance.

Rock glacier – An accumulation of coarse, angular and blocky debris at the toe of a mountain that can be metres high and wide, and up to a few kilometres long. Rock glaciers show no sign of ice at their surface, but ice may fill, or may have filled, the areas between the blocky debris. The debris is usually from a neighbouring mountain that has undergone weathering and erosion of large blocks of rock by the action of freezing and thawing water into fractures and faults. In addition, rock glaciers can develop from moraine containing a high percentage of gravel-size material. They may move slowly or be stagnant.

Rubble – A loose, unconsolidated mass of rough, angular fragments of rock broken off from larger masses of rock by natural physical forces.

S

Sand – In the classification used here, sand-sized particles are between 0.0625-02.00 mm in diameter. The shape and size of sand particles are modified by abrasion during transport by wind, water, ice or gravity. The term sand is also used to describe a bed of predominantly sand-sized particles that are loosely bound (not lithified).

Sandstone – A lithified sedimentary rock composed primarily of sand-sized particles.

Scarp – A short form of escarpment; an abrupt, vertical or near vertical slope.

Sediment – A general term applied to loose rock particles or fragments deposited by a variety of processes.

Sedimentary rock – Rock formed by the lithification of rounded to angular rock fragments eroded from other igneous, metamorphic or sedimentary rocks, or by the precipitation of minerals directly from water, and transported to the site of deposition by wind, water, ice or gravity.

Shale – A fine-grained sedimentary rock formed by the consolidation of clay, silt or mud, characterized by a finely laminated structure.

Shield – A large area of exposed rock of Precambrian age (565 million years ago and older) surrounded by young sedimentary rock platforms. The best example of this in Canada is the Precambrian Shield that covers much of the eastern and northern part of the country.

Silt – In the classification used here, silt particles are between 0.002 mm and 0.0625 mm in diameter. Silt-sized particles are not visible to the naked eye. The lower boundary of silt-sized particles is coincident with the upper boundary of clay-sized particles.

Siltstone – A lithified sedimentary rock composed mainly of silt-sized material.

Slope wash – Soil or rock material being or having been moved down a slope predominately by gravity assisted by running water not concentrated in well defined channels.

Slump – A landslide characterized by shearing and rotary movement of a generally independent mass of rock or earth along a concave, upwardly curved slip surface.

Soil – a) Engineering definition – the agglomeration of mineral and organic material extending from the ground surface down to solid rock. b) Agricultural/scientific definition – the naturally occurring, unconsolidated mineral or organic material at least 10 cm thick and capable of supporting plant growth.

Splaying Crevasse – A crevasse that is essentially parallel to glacial flow in the center of a glacier, but curves towards the margin downstream.

Stagnant glacier – A glacier that no longer flows and is ablating in place.

Stratum (plural - **strata**) – A layer of rock, usually sedimentary, separated by bedding planes.

Stoss – The opposite of lee side. The stoss side faces the direction from which a glacier moved; that is, it faces the upstream side of a glacier.

Stratified – Formed, arranged, or laid down in layers or strata.

Stream or river terrace – One or more level terraces in a stream or river valley that once marked the base of a river or a floodplain. Subsequent down cutting by the river or stream forms a new stream or river channel below the top of the terrace.

Striation – In the glacial sense, a scratch on rock made by a geological agent such as rocks frozen to the bottom of the glacier. A scratch is made by a relatively hard rock scratching a softer rock. The trend of a striation or striations on bedrock usually indicates

the down slope direction of local glacial movement.

Strike – The direction of a structural surface (bedding plane, fault plane), measured by determining the direction of a horizontal line on that surface, generally with respect to the north direction, either true or magnetic.

Supraglacial (**superglacial**) – Material carried on the surface of a glacier. Supraglacial till is derived from this material.

Surficial deposit – Generally used to describe an unconsolidated deposit formed at, and situated on the surface of the Earth and lying on bedrock.

T

Talus – A sloping mass of loose, detrital sediment lying at the base of a cliff or similar landform and consisting of material fallen from a cliff or slope face. Talus is a type of colluvium, and commonly forms a cone or fan shape.

Tephra – see Volcanic Ash.

Terminal moraine – The outermost end moraine that marks the furthest advance of a glacier during a major glacial event.

Terrace – Any long, narrow relatively level or gently inclined step-like surface, generally less broad than a plain, bounded on one side by a steep descending slope or scarp and on the other side by a steep ascending slope or scarp.

Terrain (also **terrane**) – A comprehensive term used to describe a tract of land with respect to its natural features and topography.

Till – Unsorted and unstratified glacial drift, generally unconsolidated, deposited directly by a glacier without or with minor reworking by meltwater, and consisting of

a heterogeneous mixture of clay, silt, sand, granules, pebbles, cobbles and boulders.

Transverse crevasse – A crevasse that develops across a glacier roughly perpendicular to the direction of glacial movement, commonly convex on the downstream side.

Tributary – A smaller stream, river or glacier that flows into a larger one.

Trough – A long narrow depression in the Earth's surface such as between hills and with no surface outlet for drainage.

Trough cross-bedding – Refers to cross-bedding in which the lower bounding surfaces are curved surfaces of erosion.

U

U-shaped valley – A preglacial river valley, which has been eroded by a glacier so that the valley between the hills or mountains takes on the shape similar to the letter 'U' with steep, relatively smoothed sides. In mountainous areas, the base of the valley often contains a river.

Unconsolidated – Loose material that is not lithified; generally surficial material.

V

Valley – A long depression or hollow tract of land, commonly with an outlet, between hills or mountains and formed usually by stream erosion or earth movement such as faulting or folding, or a combination of the two.

Volcanic ash – Fine material (under 2 mm diameter) derived from a volcanic eruption or explosion. Sometimes called tephra.

Selected References and Further Reading

General

Benn, D.I. and Evans, D.J.A., 1998. Glaciers and Glaciation. London, Arnold, pp. 734.

Bradley, Raymond S., 1999. Paleoclimatology: Reconstructing Climates of the Quaternary. San Diego, Academic Press, pp. 613.

Houghton, J. T., Y. Ding, D.J. Griggs, M. Noguer, P. J. van der Linden and D. Xiaosu (Eds.) 2001. Climate Change 2001: The Scientific Basis. Contribution of Working Group I to the Third Assessment Report of the Intergovernmental Panel of Climate Change. Cambridge, Cambridge University Press, pp. 944.

Lowe, J.J. and Walker, M.J.C., 1999. Reconstructing Quaternary Environments. Essex, Longman, pp. 446.

McCarthy, James J., Osvaldo F. Canziani, Neil A. Leary, David J. Dokken and Kasey S. White (Eds.), 2001. Climate Change 2001: Impacts, Adaptation and Vulnerability. Contribution of Working Group II to the Third Assessment Report of the Intergovernmental Panel of Climate Change. Cambridge, Cambridge University Press, pp. 1000.

Metz, Bert, Ogunlade Davidson, Rob Swart and Jiahua Pan (Eds.), 2001. Climate Change 2001: Mitigation. Contribution of Working Group III to the Third Assessment Report of the Intergovernmental Panel of Climate Change. Cambridge, Cambridge University Press, pp. 700.

PAGES Scientific Steering Committee, 1992. Past Global Changes Project: Proposed Implementation Plans for Research Activities. International Geosphere-Biosphere Programme. Stockholm, pp. 110.

Tungsheng Liu, Zhongli Ding and Nat Rutter.1999. Comparison of Milankovitch periods between continental loess and deep sea records over the last 2.5 Ma. Quaternary Science Reviews, vol. 18, p. 1205-1212.

Veevers, J.J., 1990. Tectonic-climatic supercycle in the billion-year plate-tectonic eon: Permian Pangean icehouse alternates with Cretaceous dispersed-continents greenhouse. Sedimentary Geology vol. 68, p. 1–16.

Glaciation of the Banff and Jasper Areas

Jackson, Jr., L., Rutter, N.W., Hughes, O.L. and Clague, J.J., 1989. Glaciated Fringe (Quaternary Stratigraphy and History, Canadian Cordillera). In: Quaternary Geology of Canada and Greenland. Edited by R.J. Fulton, Geological Survey of Canada, Geology of Canada, p. 63–68.

Rutter, N.W., 1972. Geomorphology and multiple glaciation, Banff area, Alberta. Geological Survey of Canada Bulletin 206, pp. 54.

Rutter, N.W., 1984. Pleistocene History of the Western Canada Ice-Free Corridor. In: Quaternary Stratigraphy of Canada – a Canadian Contribution of IGCP Project 24. Edited by R.J. Fulton, Geological Survey of Canada Paper 84-10, p. 49–56.

Levson, V.M., Rutter, N.W. and Luckman, B.H., 2000. Quaternary Geology of Banff and Jasper National Parks. Field Trip Guidebook No. 1, Geological Association of Canada, GeoCanada 2000, pp. 80.

Levson, V.M. and Rutter, N.W., 1995. Pleistocene stratigraphy of the Athabasca River Valley region, Rocky Mountains, Canada. Geographie Physique et Quaternaire, vol. 49, p. 381–399.

Roed, M.A., 1975. Cordilleran and Laurentide multiple glaciations, west central Alberta, Canadian Journal of Earth Sciences, vol. 12, p. 1493–1515.

Hinton Drumlins

Gambier, A.M., 1984. Glacigenic Streamlined Landforms in the Hinton/Edson Area, Alberta. M.Sc. Thesis, University of Alberta, Department of Geography, pp. 134.

Late Quaternary Environments

Beaudoin, A.B. and Kind, R.H., 1990. Late Quaternary vegetation history of Wilcox Pass, Jasper National Park, Alberta. Palaeogeography, Paleoclimatology, Palaeoecology, vol. 80, p. 129–144.

Hart, Jane K., 2006. Athabasca Glacier, Canada—a field example of subglacial ice and till erosion? Earth Surface Processes and Landforms, v. 31, p. 65–80.

Luckman, B.H., 1988. Dating the moraines and recession of Athabasca and Dome Glaciers, Alberta Canada. Arctic and Alpine Research, vol. 20, no. 1, p. 40–54.

Luckman, B.H., 1999 (ed). Fieldtrip Guidebook Columbia Icefield, Aug. 20–22, 1999. CANQUA-CGRC Meeting 1990. Calgary, pp. 86.

Luckman, B.H., 2000. The Little Ice Age in the Canadian Rockies. Geomorphology, vol. 2, p. 357–384.

Luckman, B.H. and Wilson, R.J.S., 2005. Summer temperatures in the Canadian Rockies during the last millennium: a revised record. Climate Dynamics vol. 24, p. 131–144.

Ommanney, C. Simon L., 2002. Glaciers of the Canadian Rockies, in: Richard S. Williams, Jr., and Jane G. Ferrigno (eds.) Satellite Image Atlas of Glaciers of the World, U.S. Geological Survey Prof. Paper 1386-J-1, pp. 96.

Osborn, G. and Gerlaff, L., 1997. Latest Pleistocene and Early Holocene fluctuations of glaciers in the Canadian and Northern Rockies. Quaternary International, vols. 38/39, p. 3–19.

Osborn, G.D. and Luckman, B.H., 1988. Holocene glacier fluctuations in the Canadian Cordillera, Alberta and British Columbia. Quaternary Science Reviews, vol. 7, p. 115–128.

Reasoner, M.L., 1987. The Late Quaternary lacustrine record from the upper Cataract Brook Valley, Yoho National Park, British Columbia, Alberta. M.Sc. Thesis, University of Alberta, Department of Geology, pp. 201.

Reasoner, M.L., Osborn, G. and Rutter, N.W., 1994. Age of the Crowfoot Advance in the Canadian Rocky Mountains: A glacial event coeval with the Younger Dryas oscillation. Geology, vol. 22, p. 439–442.

Landslides

Cruden, D.M., 1976. Major rockslides in the Rockies. Canadian Geotechnical Journal, vol. 13, p. 8–20.

Volcanic Ash

King, R.H. 1986. Weathering of Holocene ashes in the Southern Canadian Rockies. In: Rates of Chemical Weathering in Rocks and Minerals, S.M. Coleman and D.P. Dethier (Eds.), p.239-264. Academic Press, New York.

Westgate, J.A. and Dreimanis, A., 1967. Volcanic ash layer of Recent age in Banff National Park, Alberta, Canada. Canadian Journal of Earth Sciences, vol. 4, p. 155–161.

Westgate, J.A. and Naser, N.D., 1995. Tephrochronology and fission track dating. In: Rutter, N.W. and Catto, N.R. (eds.), Dating Methods for Quaternary Deposits. St. John's Newfoundland. Geological Association of Canada, Geotext 2.

Short-Term Climate Change

Braun, Holger and others, 2005. Possible solar origin of the 1,470-year glacial climate cycle demonstrated in a coupled model. Nature, vol. 438, p. 208–211.

Future Climate Change

Barnett, T.P., Adam, J.C. and Lettenmaier, D.P., 2005. Potential impacts of a warming climate on water availability in snow-dominated regions. Nature, vol. 438, p. 303–309.

Glossary

Bates, R.L., and J.A. Jackson, eds., 1987. Glossary of Geology, Third Edition, American Geological Institute, Alexandria, Virginia, U.S.A. pp. 788.

Kupsch, W.O. and N.W. Rutter, 1982. Mineral Terrain Terminology. Technical Memorandum No. 131, Associate Committee in Geotechnical Research, National Research Council, Ottawa, pp. 141.

Acknowledgments

The worldwide interest in climate change was greatly accelerated by the formation of the Past Global Changes Project (PAGES) of the International Geosphere-Biosphere Programme of the International Council of Scientific Unions in 1991. The senior author was a member of the steering committee of this project when the strategy and implementation were developed, and had the benefit of numerous discussions with many world experts on most topics presented in the Introduction, Archives of Climate Change, Dating the Archives, and Extracting Climate Information. We give special acknowledgement and thanks to Ray Bradley, Jack Eddy, Liu Tungsheng, Hans Oeschger, Jonathan Overpeck, Richard Peltier, Jorge Rabassa, Andre Velitchko and Ding Zhongli—all at one time were members of the PAGES Scientific Steering Committee (see Selected References and Further Readings).

The chapters on Interpreting the Last Ice Age, Finding Climate Change in the Rockies, and Glaciation in the Banff-Jasper Area are based in part on the authors' own work, but major contributions by many scientists have aided in reconstructing past climatic events. Especially beneficial were discussions through the years on the glaciation of Banff and Jasper National Parks with Peter Bobrowsky, Norm Catto, John Clague, Mark Fenton, Robert Fulton, Lionel Jackson, Jr., Rudolph Klassen, Louise Leslie, Victor Levson, Edward Little, David Liverman, Gregory Mandryk, Eric Mountjoy, Murray Roed, Charles Schweger and Brent Ward, and with Alwynne Beaudoin, Brian Luckman, Gerry Osborn and Mel Reasoner on Holocene glaciation and environments. Thanks to Dave Cruden for information on landslides and John Westgate for volcanic ash data. Andy Gambier's interpretation of the Hinton drumlins was particularly helpful. We greatly appreciate and acknowledge the help given by these scientists.

The Road Log Guide was compiled and modified by the authors over the years. Thanks go to Victor Levson and Brian Luckman for descriptions of several stops in Jasper National Park. The chapters on Short Term and Future Climate Change are based on assimilating data in the scientific and popular press and discussions with members of the Steering Committee of PAGES mentioned above, and with many others including Andrew Bush, Konstantin Dlusskiy, John Matthews, Richard Peltier, David Schindler, James Teller and Andrew Weaver, to name a few. We acknowledge and thank them for their contributions.

We are grateful to the scientists, photographers and institutions around the world that granted permission to use their photographs or data in this book. They are named individually in the Image Credits. Their willingness to assist authors whom they have not met, and in many cases to make the effort to supply high resolution images and background information, are fine examples of cooperation within the scientific community.

Randle Robertson, Executive Director of The Burgess Shale Geoscience Foundation, was a consistent supporter of this project and provided valuable advice and encouragement.

Finally, we thank Murray Larson, Christopher Rutter and Marie Rutter for reviewing and commenting on the manuscript.

Image Credits

Cover: Robert Berdan, Calgary, Alberta. Frontispiece: NASA Jet Propulsion Laboratory and University of Alaska, Fairbanks. Figure 2: after Wallace Broecker and others. Figure 3: Wayne Powell, Brooklyn College, Brooklyn, New York. Figure 4: after J.J. Veevers, 1990. Figure 5: Paleogeographic maps by C.R. Scotese, PALEOMAP Project, University of Texas at Arlington, www.scotese.com. Figure 6: after numerous public sources, including Wikipedia. Figure 7: after A.N. Strahler, 1965. Figure 8: Anne Jennings, INSTAAR and Department of Geological Sciences, University of Colorado. Figure 9: H.B. Brady, 1884. Figure 10: Jacques Descloitres, MODIS Rapid Response Team, NASA/GSFC, http://visibleearth.nasa.gov. Figure 11: Konstantin Dlusskiy and Dustin White. Figure 12: Nat Rutter. Figure 19: Gerard Wellington, University of Houston and National Oceanic and Atmospheric Administration Paleoclimatology Program, U.S. Department of Commerce. Figure 21: George Ball, University of Alberta. Figure 22: Tom Van Devender, Arizona – Sonora Desert Museum and National Oceanic and Atmospheric Administration Paleoclimatology Program, U.S. Department of Commerce. Figure 23: Pieter Brueghel the Elder, 1565, public domain. Figure 24: Frits Koek, Royal Netherlands Meteorological Institute (KNMI), The Netherlands. Figure 31: Peter Van den haute, Ghent University, Belgium. Figure 34: W.A. Bentley, 1931. Figure 35: Mark Twickler, University of New Hampshire and National Oceanic and Atmospheric Administration Paleoclimatology Program,

U.S. Department of Commerce. Figure 36: Ken Abbott, University of Colorado and National Oceanic and Atmospheric Administration Paleoclimatology Program, U.S. Department of Commerce. Figures 37 and 38: Anthony J. Gow, U.S. Army Engineer Research and Development Center, Hanover, New Hampshire and National Oceanic and Atmospheric Administration Paleoclimatology Program, U.S. Department of Commerce. Figure 39: after P.M Grootes and M. Stuiver, 1997, J. Geophys. Res. v. 102, p. 26455–26470. Figure 40: after J.R. Petit and others, 1999. Nature v. 399 p. 429–436. Figure 41: Dennis Darby, Old Dominion University, Norfolk, Virginia. Figure 42: Bedford Institute of Oceanography, Dartmouth, Nova Scotia. Figure 43: Carlos Zarikian, Texas A&M University, College Station, Texas. Figure 44: foraminifera: Antje Voelker, Instituto Nacional de Engenharia, Technologia e Inovação I.P. (INETI), Zambujal, Portugal; coiling data after Hilary Clement Olson, Institute for Geophysics, University of Texas, Austin, Texas. Figure 45: Nat Rutter. Figure 46: Liu Tungsheng, Chinese Academy of Sciences. Figure 47: National Aeronautics and Space Administration (NASA), Washington, D.C., U.S.A., http://visibleearth.nasa. gov. Figure 48: after Liu Tungsheng, Ding Zhongli and Nat Rutter, 1999. Figure 50: Paleogeographic map by C.R. Scotese, PALEOMAP Project, University of Texas at Arlington, www.scotese.com. Figure 51: ice sheet limits after A.S. Dyke, Geological Survey of Canada. Figure 63: Chris

Hopkinson, Nova Scotia Community College, Middleton, Nova Scotia. Figure 65: James Hector, 1861, Geol. Soc. London v. XVII, no. 68, p. 388–445. Figure 68: University of Alberta and NASA/GSFC/MITI/ ERSDAC/JAROS, and U.S./Japan ASTER Science Team, http://visibleearth.nasa.gov. Figures 69, 71, 72: modified false-colour satellite images; originals from LANDSAT 7. Figure 73: Travel Alberta. Figure 83: Mel Reasoner (re-drafted). Figure 85: Dan J. Smith, Department of Geography, University of Victoria, Victoria, British Columbia. Figure 90: modified after R.H. King, 1986. Figure 93: modified false-colour satellite image; original from LANDSAT 7. Figure 101: Travel Alberta. Figure 124: modified from LANDSAT 7 image. Figures 127 and 129: courtesy of David J. Skelton, Foto Flight, Calgary, Alberta. Figure 132: Travel Alberta. Figure 142: Nat Rutter. Figure 143: Jacques Descloitres, MODIS Rapid Response Team, NASA/GSFC, http://visibleearth.nasa.gov. Figure 144: NASA Goddard Space Flight Center. Figure 145: after J.R. Petit and others, 1999. Nature v. 399 p. 429–436. Figure 147: Yukon Government, courtesy of Greg Hare. Figures 149 and 150: modified from Glacier Mass Balance Bulletin No. 7 (2003), World Glacier Monitoring Service, University of Zurich, Zurich, Switzerland.

All other photographs and diagrams by Murray Coppold.

About the Authors

Nat Rutter

Nat has spent most of his career working on scientific problems concerning the Quaternary Period, the last 2.6 million years of Earth history. After graduating with his Ph.D. from the University of Alberta, he joined the Geological Survey of Canada in Calgary, spending most of his time investigating the glacial history and climate change of Western Canada. Returning to the University of Alberta as Professor and then Chairman of the Department of Geology, he and his graduate students continued climate change research not only in Canada but also in China, Siberia, Europe, Africa and South America. He is currently University Professor Emeritus of Earth and Atmospheric Sciences.

He has been a member of many scientific committees and organizations, including President of the International Union for Quaternary Research. He was one of the founding members of the international program on Past Global Change. Nat is the founder and first editor-in-chief of the scientific periodical *Quaternary International*.

His numerous honours include Fellow of the Royal Society of Canada, Officer of the Order of Canada, Honourary Doctor of Science, and Honourary Professor of the Chinese Academy of Sciences. Nat has distinguished career awards from the Geological Association of Canada, the Geological Society of America and the Canadian Quaternary Association. He is a founding member of The Burgess Shale Geoscience Foundation and a member of the Association of Professional Engineers, Geologists and Geophysicists of Alberta.

Murray Coppold

Murray graduated from McGill University with an M.Sc. in Geology and spent nearly three decades in Canadian and international petroleum exploration. He has field experience in the Rockies, the Mackenzie Mountains and the Arctic. Murray has a wide range of interests including paleontology, carbonate geology, climate change, and alpine and arctic geomorphology. He is a long-time volunteer with The Burgess Shale Geoscience Foundation and other organizations promoting science or environmental literacy.

Murray is a member of the Canadian Society of Petroleum Geologists; the Association of Professional Engineers, Geologists and Geophysicists of Alberta; and a life member of the Arctic Institute of North America and the Canadian Arctic Resources Committee.

Dean Rokosh

Dean was born and raised in Saskatchewan until his family moved to Alberta in 1967. Dean graduated from the Southern Alberta Institute of Technology in 1977 and worked as a geological technologist for 12 years in the petroleum industry in Calgary for Hudson's Bay Oil and Gas, Dome Petroleum and Amoco Petroleum. In 1990 Dean enrolled at the University of Alberta and graduated with a B.Sc. in Geology in 1994 and a Ph.D. in Quaternary Geology in 2001. His thesis topic was past climate changes interpreted from loess and paleosol sequences from the Central Loess Plateau of China. This was followed by three years as a post-doctorate fellow in the Department of Physics at the University of Alberta.

He has a broad base of expertise and interests in geology and climate studies including paleoclimate, stratigraphy, sedimentation, Quaternary surficial geology and oil and gas subsurface geology. Dean is a member of the Canadian Society of Petroleum Geologists, and is currently employed at the Energy and Utilities Board / Alberta Geological Survey.

Index

P

paleoclimate 10, 15, 17, 135

paleosol 11, 30, 35, 38–39, 73, 105, 125

paleotemperature 6, 13, 17, 28–29, 70, 72

permafrost 4, 116

plate tectonics 3, 7

Pleistocene 39, 40, 438

pollen 14, 18, 67–69

proxy 9, 16, 29, 32, 39, 111, 113

Q

Quaternary 1, 4, 8, 38–39, 45, 108

R

radiocarbon 14, 16, 18, 23–24, 39, 45, 63, 67, 71, 74–75, 81, 89–91, 103, 105

rock flour 83, 89

rock glacier 71, 72, 92

S

safety 94

snowpack 114, 115

speleothems 16, 17

sunspots 110

T

talus slopes 52, 73

thermohaline 3, 111

till 50–52, 54, 57–58, 60, 62–66, 78, 80–81, 103–104, 106–107, 117, 121–124, 126

timberline 114–115

tree ring 15–17, 24, 67 70–71

U

uranium 16–17, 22, 24–25

V

varves 14, 27

W

Wisconsinan 31, 42–43, 56–60, 62–65, 67, 78, 103–104

Y

Younger Dryas 31, 39, 67–68, 89, 108–109, 111